I0448154

February 2013

FINANCIAL AUDIT

Federal Deposit Insurance Corporation Funds' 2012 and 2011 Financial Statements

G A O
Accountability ★ Integrity ★ Reliability

GAO-13-291

February 2013

FINANCIAL AUDIT

Federal Deposit Insurance Corporation Funds' 2012 and 2011 Financial Statements

GAO

Accountability * Integrity * Reliability

Highlights

Highlights of GAO-13-291, a report to congressional committees

Why GAO Did This Study

Created in 1933 to insure bank deposits and promote sound banking practices, FDIC plays an important role in maintaining public confidence in the nation's financial system. FDIC administers the DIF, which protects bank and savings deposits, and the FRF, which was created to close out the business of the former Federal Savings and Loan Insurance Corporation (FSLIC).

GAO annually audits the financial statements of the DIF and the FRF pursuant to Section 17 of the Federal Deposit Insurance Act, as amended, and the Government Corporation Control Act. GAO is responsible for obtaining reasonable assurance about whether (1) FDIC's financial statements for the DIF and the FRF are presented fairly in all material respects, in accordance with U.S. generally accepted accounting principles; (2) FDIC maintained effective internal control over financial reporting; and (3) there are any reportable instances of FDIC noncompliance with tested provisions of laws and regulations.

What GAO Recommends

GAO is not making recommendations in this report. In commenting on a draft of this report, FDIC stated that it recognizes the important role a strong internal control program plays in achieving the agency's mission, and its dedication to establishing sound financial management has been and will remain a top priority.

View GAO-13-291. For more information, contact James R. Dalkin at (202) 512-3133 or dalkinj@gao.gov.

What GAO Found

In GAO's opinion, the Federal Deposit Insurance Corporation (FDIC) fairly presented, in all material respects, the 2012 and 2011 financial statements for the two funds it administers—the Deposit Insurance Fund (DIF) and the FSLIC Resolution Fund (FRF). Also, in GAO's opinion, FDIC maintained, in all material respects, effective internal control over financial reporting relevant to the DIF and the FRF as of December 31, 2012. Further, GAO did not find any reportable instances of noncompliance with provisions of the laws and regulations it tested.

The banking industry continued to recover in 2012. During 2012, 51 insured institutions with combined assets of $11.8 billion failed. The losses to the DIF from failures that occurred in 2012 were lower than the amount reserved at the end of 2011. This occurred primarily because the aggregate number and size of institution failures in 2012—and their estimated cost to the DIF—were less than anticipated. As discussed in note 17 to the DIF's financial statements, through February 14, 2013, two institutions have failed thus far during 2013. As of December 31, 2012, the DIF had a fund balance of $33 billion, compared to a fund balance of $11.8 billion at December 31, 2011. DIF's ratio of reserves to estimated insured deposits as of the end of September of 2012 was 0.35 percent, compared to 0.17 percent at the end of 2011. FDIC's long range target is to maintain the reserve ratio at a minimum 2 percent.

In an effort to counter the system-wide crisis in the nation's financial sector, the FDIC established the Temporary Liquidity Guarantee Program (TLGP) on October 14, 2008, for insured depository institutions, designated affiliates and certain holding companies. At its inception, the TLGP consisted of two components: 1) the Transaction Account Guarantee Program (TAG) and 2) the Debt Guarantee Program (DGP). The TAG provided unlimited coverage for noninterest-bearing transaction accounts held by insured depository institutions on all deposit amounts exceeding the fully insured limit of $250,000 through December 31, 2010. The DGP permitted participating entities to issue FDIC-guaranteed senior unsecured debt. The FDIC's guarantee for all such debt expired on December 31, 2012. The expiration of the guarantee period for the DGP marked the conclusion of the TLGP. As established under terms of the TLGP, all excess funds were transferred to the DIF.

Contents

Abbreviations

CFO	Chief Financial Officer
DGP	Debt Guarantee Program
DIF	Deposit Insurance Fund
FDIC	Federal Deposit Insurance Corporation
FMFIA	Federal Managers' Financial Integrity Act of 1982
FRF	FSLIC Resolution Fund
FSLIC	Federal Savings and Loan Insurance Corporation
TAG	Transaction Account Guarantee Program
TLGP	Temporary Liquidity Guarantee Program

February 21, 2013

The Honorable Tim Johnson
Chairman
The Honorable Mike Crapo
Ranking Member
Committee on Banking, Housing, and Urban Affairs
United States Senate

The Honorable Jeb Hensarling
Chairman
The Honorable Maxine Waters
Ranking Member
Committee on Financial Services
House of Representatives

This report presents the results of our audits of the financial statements of
the Deposit Insurance Fund (DIF) and the FSLIC Resolution Fund (FRF)
as of, and for the years ending December 31, 2012, and 2011. These
financial statements are the responsibility of the Federal Deposit
Insurance Corporation (FDIC), the administrator of the two funds.

This report contains our (1) opinion that the financial statements of the DIF
and the FRF are fairly presented, in all material respects; (2) opinion that
FDIC maintained, in all material respects, effective internal control over
financial reporting relevant to the DIF and the FRF as of December 31,
2012; and (3) conclusion that we found no reportable compliance issues
during 2012 with provisions of laws and regulations we tested.

We are sending copies of this report to the Chairman of the Board of
Directors of FDIC; the Chairman of the FDIC Audit Committee; the
Chairman of the Board of Governors of the Federal Reserve System; the
Comptroller of the Currency; the Secretary of the Treasury; the Director of
the Office of Management and Budget; and other interested parties. In
addition, this report will be available at no charge on GAO's website at
http://www.gao.gov.

If you have any questions concerning this report, please contact me at
(202) 512-3133 or dalkinj@gao.gov. Contact points for our Offices of

Congressional Relations and Public Affairs may be found on the last page of this report.

James R. Dalkin
Director
Financial Management and Assurance

United States Government Accountability Office
Washington, D.C. 20548

Independent Auditor's Report

To the Board of Directors
The Federal Deposit Insurance Corporation

In our audits of the 2012 and 2011 financial statements of the Deposit Insurance Fund (DIF) and the FSLIC Resolution Fund (FRF), both of which are administered by the Federal Deposit Insurance Corporation (FDIC)[1], we found

- the financial statements of the DIF and the FRF as of and for the years ended December 31, 2012, and 2011, are presented fairly, in all material respects, in accordance with U.S. generally accepted accounting principles;

- FDIC maintained, in all material respects, effective internal control over financial reporting relevant to the DIF and the FRF as of December 31, 2012; and

- no reportable noncompliance with provisions of laws and regulations we tested.

The following sections discuss in more detail (1) our reports on the financial statements and internal control, including two matters of emphasis related to improvements in the banking industry's and the DIF's financial condition, and the expiration of the Temporary Liquidity Guarantee Program; (2) our report on compliance with laws and regulations; and (3) agency comments and our evaluation.

Reports on the Financial Statements and Internal Control

In accordance with Section 17 of the Federal Deposit Insurance Act, as amended, and the Government Corporation Control Act, we have audited the financial statements of the DIF and FRF, both of which are administered by FDIC. The DIF statements comprise the balance sheets as of December 31, 2012 and 2011; the related statements of income and fund balance, and cash flows for the years then ended; and the related

---

[1] A third fund managed by FDIC, the Orderly Liquidation Fund, established by Section 210 of the Dodd-Frank Wall Street Reform and Consumer Protection Act, Pub. L. No. 111-203, 124 Stat. 1376, 1506 (July 21, 2010), is unfunded and did not have any transactions during 2012 or 2011.

notes to the financial statements. The FRF statements comprise the balance sheets as of December 31, 2012 and 2011; the related statements of income and accumulated deficit, and cash flows for the years then ended; and the related notes to the financial statements. We also have audited FDIC's internal control over financial reporting relevant to the DIF and the FRF as of December 31, 2012, based on criteria established under 31 U.S.C. § 3512(c), (d), commonly known as the Federal Managers' Financial Integrity Act of 1982 (FMFIA).

We conducted our audits in accordance with U.S. generally accepted government auditing standards. We believe that the audit evidence we obtained is sufficient and appropriate to provide a basis for our audit opinions.

Management's Responsibility

FDIC management is responsible for (1) the preparation and fair presentation of these financial statements in accordance with U.S. generally accepted accounting principles; (2) maintaining effective internal control over financial reporting, including the design, implementation, and maintenance of internal control relevant to the preparation and fair presentation of financial statements that are free from material misstatement, whether due to fraud or error; (3) evaluating the effectiveness of internal control over financial reporting based on the criteria established under FMFIA; and (4) providing its assertion about the effectiveness of internal control over financial reporting as of December 31, 2012, based on its evaluation, included in the accompanying Management Report on Internal Control over Financial Reporting in Appendix 1.

Auditor's Responsibility

Our responsibility is to express opinions on these financial statements and opinions on FDIC's internal control over financial reporting relevant to the DIF and the FRF based on our audits. U.S. generally accepted government auditing standards require that we plan and perform the audits to obtain reasonable assurance about whether the financial statements are free from material misstatement, and whether effective internal control over financial reporting was maintained in all material respects as of December 31, 2012.

An audit of financial statements involves performing procedures to obtain audit evidence about the amounts and disclosures in the financial statements. The procedures selected depend on the auditor's judgment, including the auditor's assessment of the risks of material misstatement of the financial statements, whether due to fraud or error. In making those risk assessments, the auditor considers internal control relevant to the entity's preparation and fair presentation of the financial statements in order to design audit procedures that are appropriate in the circumstances. An audit of financial statements also involves evaluating the appropriateness of the accounting policies used and the reasonableness of significant accounting estimates made by management, as well as evaluating the overall presentation of the financial statements. An audit of internal control over financial reporting includes obtaining an understanding of internal control over financial reporting, assessing the risk that a material weakness exists, evaluating the design and operating effectiveness of internal control based on the assessed risk, and testing relevant internal control over financial reporting. Our audit of internal control also considered the entity's process for evaluating and reporting on internal control over financial reporting based on criteria established under FMFIA. Our audits also included performing such other procedures as we considered necessary in the circumstances.

We did not evaluate all internal controls relevant to operating objectives as broadly established under FMFIA, such as those controls relevant to preparing performance information and ensuring efficient operations. We limited our internal control testing to testing controls over financial reporting. Our internal control testing was for the purpose of expressing an opinion on whether effective internal control over financial reporting was maintained, in all material respects. Consequently, our audit may not identify all deficiencies in internal control over financial reporting that are less severe than a material weakness.[2]

Definitions and Inherent Limitations of Internal Control

An entity's internal control over financial reporting is a process effected by those charged with governance, management, and other personnel, the objectives of which are to provide reasonable assurance that (1) transactions are properly recorded, processed, and summarized to permit the preparation of financial statements in accordance with U.S. generally

---

[2]A material weakness is a deficiency, or combination of deficiencies, in internal control over financial reporting such that there is a reasonable possibility that a material misstatement of the entity's financial statements will not be prevented or detected and corrected on a timely basis. A deficiency in internal control exists when the design or operation of a control does not allow management or employees, in the normal course of performing their assigned functions, to prevent or detect and correct misstatements on a timely basis.

accepted accounting principles, and assets are safeguarded against loss from unauthorized acquisition, use, or disposition; and (2) transactions are executed in accordance with laws and regulations that could have a direct and material effect on the financial statements.

Because of its inherent limitations, internal control over financial reporting may not prevent, or detect and correct misstatements due to fraud or error. We also caution that projecting any evaluation of effectiveness to future periods is subject to the risk that controls may become inadequate because of changes in conditions, or that the degree of compliance with the policies or procedures may deteriorate.

Opinions

In our opinion:

- The DIF's financial statements present fairly, in all material respects, the DIF's financial position as of December 31, 2012, and 2011; the results of its operations; and its cash flows for the years then ended, in accordance with U.S. generally accepted accounting principles.

- The FRF's financial statements present fairly, in all material respects, the FRF's financial position as of December 31, 2012, and 2011; the results of its operations; and its cash flows for the years then ended, in accordance with U.S generally accepted accounting principles.

- FDIC maintained, in all material respects, effective internal control over financial reporting relevant to the DIF as of December 31, 2012, based on criteria established under FMFIA.

- FDIC maintained, in all material respects, effective internal control over financial reporting relevant to the FRF as of December 31, 2012, based on criteria established under FMFIA.

In our 2011 audit report[3] we reported a significant deficiency[4] concerning the effectiveness of controls over FDIC's process for deriving and

---

[3]GAO, Financial Audit: Federal Deposit Insurance Corporation Funds' 2011 and 2010 Financial Statements, GAO-12-416, (Washington, D.C.: Apr. 19, 2012).

[4]A significant deficiency is a deficiency, or combination of deficiencies, in internal control that is less severe than a material weakness, yet important enough to merit the attention of those charged with governance.

reporting estimates of losses to the DIF from resolution transactions involving shared loss agreements.[5] During 2012, FDIC corrected the underlying control issues that constituted the significant deficiency.

During our 2012 audit, we identified deficiencies in FDIC's internal control that we do not consider to be material weaknesses or significant deficiencies. Nonetheless, these deficiencies warrant FDIC management's attention. We have communicated these matters to FDIC management and, where appropriate, will report on them separately.

Emphasis of Matters

Improvement in the Banking Industry's and the DIF's Financial Condition

As discussed in note 8 to DIF's financial statements, the banking industry continued to recover in 2012. During 2012, 51 insured institutions with combined assets of $11.8 billion failed. The losses to the DIF from failures that occurred in 2012 were lower than the amount reserved at the end of 2011, as the aggregate number and size of institution failures in 2012—and their estimated cost to the DIF—were less than anticipated. DIF's contingent liability for anticipated failures declined from $6.5 billion at December 31, 2011 to $3.2 billion at December 31, 2012. As discussed in note 17 to the DIF's financial statements, through February 14, 2013, two institutions have failed thus far during 2013.

As of December 31, 2012, the DIF had a fund balance of $33 billion, compared to a fund balance of $11.8 billion at December 31, 2011. The DIF's ratio of reserves to estimated insured deposits as of the end of September of 2012 was 0.35 percent, compared to 0.17 percent at the end of 2011. This improvement was primarily attributable to increased revenue in 2012 and, as noted above, lower losses from failed institutions than estimated at December 31, 2011, and a reduction in estimated losses from anticipated failures at December 31, 2012. FDIC'S long-range target is to maintain the reserve ratio at a minimum 2 percent.

---

[5]Under shared loss agreements FDIC sells a failed institution to an acquirer with an agreement that FDIC, through the DIF, will share in any losses the acquirer experiences in servicing and disposing of assets purchased and covered under the shared loss agreement. Typically these agreements are structured such that FDIC assumes 80 percent of any such losses.

| Expiration of the Temporary Liquidity Guarantee Program | As discussed in note 16 to the DIF's financial statements, in an effort to counter the system-wide crisis in the nation's financial sector, FDIC established the Temporary Liquidity Guarantee Program (TLGP) on October 14, 2008, for insured depository institutions, designated affiliates and certain holding companies. At its inception, the TLGP consisted of two components: (1) the Transaction Account Guarantee Program (TAG) and (2) the Debt Guarantee Program (DGP). The TAG provided unlimited coverage for noninterest-bearing transaction accounts held by insured depository institutions on all deposit amounts exceeding the fully insured limit of $250,000 through December 31, 2010. The DGP permitted participating entities to issue FDIC-guaranteed senior unsecured debt through October 31, 2009. FDIC's guarantee for all such debt expired on December 31, 2012. The expiration of the guarantee period for the DGP marked the conclusion of the TLGP. As established under terms of the TLGP, all excess funds were transferred to the DIF. Accordingly, in 2012, the DIF recognized total "Other revenue" of $5.9 billion related to the TLGP. This revenue consisted of $5.2 billion of cash and a net receivable of $693 million included in "Receivables from resolutions, net." The net receivable represents estimated recoveries on payments made under the TLGP to cover obligations.

Our opinion on the DIF's financial statements is not modified with respect to these matters. |

Report on Compliance with Laws and Regulations

In connection with our audits of the financial statements of the DIF and the FRF, both of which are administered by the FDIC, we have tested compliance with selected provisions of laws and regulations that have a direct and material effect on the DIF and FRF financial statements. We performed our tests of compliance in accordance with U.S. generally accepted government auditing standards.

| Management's Responsibility | FDIC management is responsible for complying with applicable laws and regulations. |

| Auditor's Responsibility | Our responsibility is to test compliance with selected provisions of laws and regulations that have a direct and material effect on the financial statements. We did not test compliance with all laws and regulations applicable to FDIC. We limited our tests of compliance to selected |

provisions of laws and regulations that have a direct and material effect on the financial statements for the year ended December 31, 2012. We caution that noncompliance may occur and not be detected by these tests.

Compliance with Laws and Regulations

Our tests for compliance with selected provisions of laws and regulations disclosed no instances of noncompliance that would be reportable under U.S. generally accepted government auditing standards. However, the objective of our audits was not to provide an opinion on overall compliance with laws and regulations. Accordingly, we do not express such an opinion.

Intended Purpose of Report on Compliance with Laws and Regulations

The purpose of this report is solely to describe the scope of our testing of compliance with laws and regulations, and the results of that testing, and not to provide an opinion on compliance with laws and regulations. This report is an integral part of an audit performed in accordance with U.S. generally accepted government auditing standards in considering compliance with laws and regulations. Accordingly, this report on compliance with laws and regulations is not suitable for any other purpose.

FDIC Comments and Our Evaluation

In commenting on a draft of this report, the FDIC's Chief Financial Officer (CFO) noted that the agency was pleased that we provided unmodified (unqualified) opinions on the DIF and FRF financial statements and that we reported that it had effective internal control over financial reporting and complied with tested provisions of laws and regulations.

FDIC's CFO also stated that FDIC is pleased that we acknowledged the agency's efforts to resolve the prior year significant deficiency related to estimating losses to DIF from shared-loss agreements. He also commented that FDIC will continue to focus on strengthening and improving its internal control environment, and that FDIC will continue its dedication to establishing sound financial management as a top priority in helping achieve the agency's mission.

James R. Dalkin
Director
Financial Management and Assurance

February 14, 2013

Deposit Insurance Fund's Financial Statements

Balance Sheet

DEPOSIT INSURANCE FUND (DIF)

Federal Deposit Insurance Corporation
Deposit Insurance Fund Balance Sheet at December 31
DOLLARS IN THOUSANDS

		2012		2011
Assets				
Cash and cash equivalents	$	3,100,361	$	3,277,839
Cash and investments - restricted - systemic risk (Note 16)				
(Includes cash/cash equivalents of $0 at December 31, 2012		0		4,827,319
and $1,627,073 at December 31, 2011)				
Investment in U.S. Treasury obligations, net (Note 3)		34,868,688		33,863,245
Trust preferred securities (Note 5)		2,263,983		2,213,231
Assessments receivable, net (Note 9)		1,006,852		282,247
Receivables and other assets - systemic risk (Note 16)		0		1,948,151
Interest receivable on investments and other assets, net		433,592		488,179
Receivables from resolutions, net (Note 4)		23,119,554		28,548,396
Property and equipment, net (Note 6)		392,880		401,915
Total Assets	**$**	**65,185,910**	**$**	**75,850,522**
Liabilities				
Accounts payable and other liabilities	$	349,620	$	374,164
Unearned revenue - prepaid assessments (Note 9)		1,576,417		17,399,828
Refunds of prepaid assessments (Note 9)		5,675,199		0
Liabilities due to resolutions (Note 7)		21,173,785		32,790,512
Debt Guarantee Program liabilities - systemic risk (Note 16)		0		117,027
Deferred revenue - systemic risk (Note 16)		0		6,639,954
Postretirement benefit liability (Note 13)		224,225		187,968
Contingent liabilities for:				
Anticipated failure of insured institutions (Note 8)		3,220,697		6,511,321
Systemic risk (Note 16)		0		2,216
Litigation losses (Note 8)		8,200		1,000
Total Liabilities		**32,228,143**		**64,023,990**
Commitments and off-balance-sheet exposure (Note 14)				
Fund Balance				
Accumulated Net Income		32,682,237		11,560,990
Accumulated Other Comprehensive Income				
Unrealized gain on U.S. Treasury investments, net (Note 3)		33,819		47,697
Unrealized postretirement benefit loss (Note 13)		(60,448)		(33,562)
Unrealized gain on trust preferred securities (Note 5)		302,159		251,407
Total Accumulated Other Comprehensive Income		**275,530**		**265,542**
Total Fund Balance		**32,957,767**		**11,826,532**
Total Liabilities and Fund Balance	**$**	**65,185,910**	**$**	**75,850,522**

The accompanying notes are an integral part of these financial statements.

Statement of Income and Fund Balance

DEPOSIT INSURANCE FUND (DIF)

Federal Deposit Insurance Corporation

Deposit Insurance Fund Statement of Income and Fund Balance for the Years Ended December 31

DOLLARS IN THOUSANDS

		2012		2011
Revenue				
Assessments (Note 9)	$	12,397,022	$	13,498,587
Interest on U.S. Treasury obligations		159,214		127,621
Systemic risk revenue (Note 16)		(161,135)		(131,141)
Other revenue (Note 10)		6,127,211		2,846,929
Total Revenue		**18,522,312**		**16,341,996**
Expenses and Losses				
Operating expenses (Note 11)		1,777,513		1,625,351
Systemic risk expenses (Note 16)		(161,135)		(131,141)
Provision for insurance losses (Note 12)		(4,222,595)		(4,413,629)
Insurance and other expenses		7,282		3,996
Total Expenses and Losses		**(2,598,935)**		**(2,915,423)**
Net Income		**21,121,247**		**19,257,419**
Other Comprehensive Income				
Unrealized (loss) gain on U.S. Treasury investments, net		(13,878)		20,999
Unrealized postretirement benefit loss (Note 13)		(26,886)		(15,059)
Unrealized gain (loss) on trust preferred securities (Note 5)		50,752		(84,587)
Total Other Comprehensive Income (Loss)		**9,988**		**(78,647)**
Comprehensive Income		**21,131,235**		**19,178,772**
Fund Balance - Beginning		**11,826,532**		**(7,352,240)**
Fund Balance - Ending	$	**32,957,767**	$	**11,826,532**

The accompanying notes are an integral part of these financial statements.

Statement of Cash Flows

DEPOSIT INSURANCE FUND (DIF)

Federal Deposit Insurance Corporation

Deposit Insurance Fund Statement of Cash Flows for the Years Ended December 31

DOLLARS IN THOUSANDS

	2012	2011
Operating Activities		
Net Income:	$ 21,121,247	$ 19,257,419
Adjustments to reconcile net income to net cash (used by)		
operating activities:		
Amortization of U.S. Treasury obligations	854,195	388,895
Treasury Inflation-Protected Securities inflation adjustment	(98,050)	(25,307)
Depreciation on property and equipment	76,365	77,720
Loss on retirement of property and equipment	14	1,326
Provision for insurance losses	(4,222,595)	(4,413,629)
Unrealized Loss on postretirement benefits	(26,886)	(15,059)
Change in Operating Assets and Liabilities (Net of Provision for Losses):		
(Increase) in assessments receivable, net	(724,605)	(64,354)
Decrease (Increase) in interest receivable and other assets	51,181	(227,962)
Decrease (Increase) in receivables from resolutions	6,371,418	(5,802,003)
Decrease in receivables - systemic risk	1,948,151	321,271
(Decrease) in accounts payable and other liabilities	(24,543)	(140,123)
Increase in postretirement benefit liability	36,258	22,094
(Decrease) in contingent liabilities - systemic risk	(2,216)	(117,777)
(Decrease) in contingent liabilities - litigation losses	0	(276,000)
(Decrease) Increase in liabilities due to resolutions	(11,616,727)	2,278,635
(Decrease) Increase in Debt Guarantee Program liabilities - systemic risk	(117,027)	87,693
(Decrease) in unearned revenue - prepaid assessments	(15,823,411)	(12,657,206)
(Decrease) in deferred revenue - systemic risk	(6,513,828)	(2,399,644)
Increase in refunds of prepaid assessments	5,675,199	0
Net Cash (Used) by Operating Activities	**(3,035,860)**	**(3,704,011)**
Investing Activities		
Provided by:		
Maturity of U.S. Treasury obligations	32,132,623	12,976,273
Sale of U.S. Treasury obligations	2,554,781	0
Used by:		
Purchase of property and equipment	(67,344)	(64,896)
Purchase of U.S. Treasury obligations	(33,388,751)	(36,409,429)
Net Cash Provided (Used) by Investing Activities	**1,231,309**	**(23,498,052)**
Net (Decrease) in Cash and Cash Equivalents	**(1,804,551)**	**(27,202,063)**
Cash and Cash Equivalents - Beginning	**4,904,912**	**32,106,975**
Unrestricted Cash and Cash Equivalents - Ending	**3,100,361**	**3,277,839**
Restricted Cash and Cash Equivalents - Ending	**0**	**1,627,073**
Cash and Cash Equivalents - Ending	**$ 3,100,361**	**$ 4,904,912**

The accompanying notes are an integral part of these financial statements.

NOTES TO THE FINANCIAL STATEMENTS

DEPOSIT INSURANCE FUND
December 31, 2012 and 2011

1. Operations of the Deposit Insurance Fund

OVERVIEW

The Federal Deposit Insurance Corporation (FDIC) is the independent deposit insurance agency created by Congress in 1933 to maintain stability and public confidence in the nation's banking system. Provisions that govern the operations of the FDIC are generally found in the Federal Deposit Insurance (FDI) Act, as amended (12 U.S.C. 1811, *et seq*). In carrying out the purposes of the FDI Act, the FDIC, as administrator of the Deposit Insurance Fund (DIF), insures the deposits of banks and savings associations (insured depository institutions) from loss due to institution failures. In cooperation with other federal and state agencies, the FDIC promotes the safety and soundness of insured depository institutions by identifying, monitoring and addressing risks to the DIF. Commercial banks, savings banks and savings associations (known as "thrifts") are supervised by either the FDIC, the Office of the Comptroller of the Currency, or the Federal Reserve Board.

The FDIC is also the administrator of the FSLIC Resolution Fund (FRF). The FRF is a resolution fund responsible for the sale of remaining assets and satisfaction of liabilities associated with the former Federal Savings and Loan Insurance Corporation (FSLIC) and the former Resolution Trust Corporation. The DIF and the FRF are maintained separately by the FDIC to support their respective functions.

Pursuant to the Dodd Frank Wall Street Reform and Consumer Protection Act of 2010 (Dodd Frank Act), the FDIC is the manager of the Orderly Liquidation Fund (OLF). Established as a separate fund in the U.S. Treasury (Treasury), the OLF is inactive and unfunded until the FDIC is appointed as receiver for a covered financial company (a failing financial company, such as a bank holding company or nonbank financial company for which a systemic risk determination has been made as set forth in section 203 of the Dodd Frank Act).

The Dodd Frank Act granted the FDIC authority to establish a widely available program to guarantee obligations of solvent insured depository institutions (IDIs) or solvent depository institution holding companies (including affiliates) upon the systemic determination of a liquidity event during times of severe economic distress. The program would not be funded by the DIF but rather by fees and assessments paid by all participants in the program. If fees are insufficient to cover losses or expenses, the FDIC must impose a special assessment on participants as necessary to cover the shortfall. Any excess funds at the end of the liquidity event program would be deposited in the General Fund of the Treasury. The Dodd Frank Act limits the FDIC's systemic risk determination authority under section 13 of the FDI Act to IDIs for which the FDIC has been appointed receiver. Prior to this change, the authority permitted open bank assistance and the creation of the Temporary Liquidity Guarantee Program (TLGP) that expired on December 31, 2012 (see Note 16).

1

DIF

The Dodd Frank Act also created the Financial Stability Oversight Council (FSOC) of which the Chairman of the FDIC is a member and expanded the FDIC's responsibilities to include supervisory review of resolution plans (known as living wills) and backup examination authority for systemically important bank holding companies and nonbank financial companies. The living wills provide for an entity's rapid and orderly resolution in the event of material financial distress or failure.

OPERATIONS OF THE DIF
The primary purposes of the DIF are to 1) insure the deposits and protect the depositors of IDIs and 2) resolve failed IDIs upon appointment of the FDIC as receiver, in a manner that will result in the least possible cost to the DIF (unless a systemic risk determination is made).

The DIF is primarily funded from deposit insurance assessments. Other available funding sources, if necessary, are borrowings from the Treasury, the Federal Financing Bank (FFB), Federal Home Loan Banks, and IDIs. The FDIC has borrowing authority of $100 billion from the Treasury and a Note Purchase Agreement with the FFB, not to exceed $100 billion, to enhance the DIF's ability to fund deposit insurance.

A statutory formula, known as the Maximum Obligation Limitation (MOL), limits the amount of obligations the DIF can incur to the sum of its cash, 90 percent of the fair market value of other assets, and the amount authorized to be borrowed from the Treasury. The MOL for the DIF was $132.9 billion and $114.4 billion as of December 31, 2012 and 2011, respectively.

OPERATIONS OF RESOLUTION ENTITIES
The FDIC is responsible for managing and disposing of the assets of failed institutions in an orderly and efficient manner. The assets held by receiverships, pass through conservatorships, and bridge institutions (collectively, resolution entities), and the claims against them, are accounted for separately from the DIF assets and liabilities to ensure that proceeds from these entities are distributed in accordance with applicable laws and regulations. Accordingly, income and expenses attributable to resolution entities are accounted for as transactions of those entities. Resolution entities are billed by the FDIC for services provided on their behalf.

2. Summary of Significant Accounting Policies

GENERAL
These financial statements pertain to the financial position, results of operations, and cash flows of the DIF and are presented in accordance with U.S. generally accepted accounting principles (GAAP). As permitted by the Federal Accounting Standards Advisory Board's Statement of Federal Financial Accounting Standards 34, *The Hierarchy of Generally Accepted Accounting Principles, Including the Application of Standards Issued by the Financial Accounting Standards Board*, the FDIC prepares financial statements in accordance with standards promulgated by the Financial Accounting Standards Board (FASB). These statements do not include reporting for assets and liabilities of resolution entities because these entities are legally separate and distinct, and the DIF does not have any ownership interests in them. Periodic and final accountability reports of resolution entities are furnished to courts, supervisory authorities, and others upon

2

DIF

request.

USE OF ESTIMATES
Management makes estimates and assumptions that affect the amounts reported in the financial statements and accompanying notes. Actual results could differ from these estimates. Where it is reasonably possible that changes in estimates will cause a material change in the financial statements in the near term, the nature and extent of such potential changes in estimates have been disclosed. The more significant estimates include the valuation of trust preferred securities; the assessments receivable and associated revenue; the allowance for loss on receivables from resolutions (including shared loss agreements); guarantee obligations for structured transactions; refunds of prepaid assessments; the postretirement benefit obligation; and the estimated losses for anticipated failures, litigation, and representations and indemnifications.

CASH EQUIVALENTS
Cash equivalents are short term, highly liquid investments consisting primarily of U.S. Treasury Overnight Certificates.

INVESTMENT IN U.S. TREASURY OBLIGATIONS
The DIF funds are required to be invested in obligations of the United States or in obligations guaranteed as to principal and interest by the United States. The Secretary of the Treasury must approve all such investments in excess of $100,000 and has granted the FDIC approval to invest the DIF funds only in U.S. Treasury obligations that are purchased or sold exclusively through the Bureau of the Public Debt's Government Account Series program.

The DIF's investments in U.S. Treasury obligations are classified as available for sale. Securities designated as available for sale are shown at fair value. Unrealized gains and losses are reported as other comprehensive income. Realized gains and losses are included in the Statement of Income and Fund Balance as components of net income. Income on securities is calculated and recorded on a daily basis using the effective interest or straight line method depending on the maturity of the security.

REVENUE RECOGNITION FOR ASSESSMENTS
Assessment revenue is recognized for the quarterly period of insurance coverage based on an estimate. The estimate is derived from an institution's risk based assessment rate and assessment base for the prior quarter adjusted for the current quarter's available assessment credits, certain changes in supervisory examination ratings for larger institutions, and a modest assessment base growth factor. At the subsequent quarter end, the estimated revenue amounts are adjusted when actual assessments for the covered period are determined for each institution (see Note 9).

CAPITAL ASSETS AND DEPRECIATION
The FDIC buildings are depreciated on a straight line basis over a 35 to 50 year estimated life. Leasehold improvements are capitalized and depreciated over the lesser of the remaining life of the lease or the estimated useful life of the improvements, if determined to be material. Capital assets depreciated on a straight line basis over a five year estimated useful life include mainframe equipment; furniture, fixtures, and general equipment; and internal use software. Personal computer equipment is depreciated on a straight line basis over a three year estimated useful life.

3

DIF

REPORTING ON VARIABLE INTEREST ENTITIES

FDIC receiverships engaged in structured transactions, some of which resulted in the issuance of note obligations that were guaranteed by the FDIC in its corporate capacity (see Note 8, Contingent Liabilities for: FDIC Guaranteed Debt of Structured Transactions). As the guarantor of note obligations for several structured transactions, the FDIC in its corporate capacity is the holder of a variable interest in a number of variable interest entities (VIEs). The FDIC conducts a qualitative assessment of its relationship with each VIE as required by Accounting Standards Codification (ASC) Topic 810, *Consolidation*. These assessments are conducted to determine if the FDIC in its corporate capacity has 1) power to direct the activities that most significantly impact the economic performance of the VIE and 2) an obligation to absorb losses of the VIE or the right to receive benefits from the VIE that could potentially be significant to the VIE. When a variable interest holder has met both of these characteristics, the enterprise is considered the primary beneficiary and must consolidate the VIE. In accordance with the provisions of ASC 810, an assessment of the terms of the legal agreement for each VIE was conducted to determine whether any of the terms had been activated or modified in a manner which would cause the FDIC in its corporate capacity to be characterized as a primary beneficiary. In making that determination, consideration was given to which, if any, activities were significant to each VIE. Often, the right to service collateral, to liquidate collateral, or to unilaterally dissolve the limited liability company (LLC) or trust was determined to be the most significant activity. In other cases, it was determined that the structured transactions did not include such significant activities and that the design of the entity was the best indicator of which party was the primary beneficiary. The results of each analysis identified a party other than the FDIC in its corporate capacity as the primary beneficiary.

The conclusion of these analyses was that the FDIC in its corporate capacity has not engaged in any activity that would cause the FDIC in its corporate capacity to be characterized as a primary beneficiary to any VIE with which it was involved as of December 31, 2012 and 2011. Therefore, consolidation is not required for the 2012 and 2011 DIF financial statements. In the future, the FDIC in its corporate capacity may become the primary beneficiary upon the activation of provisional contract rights that extend to the Corporation if payments are made on guarantee claims. Ongoing analyses will be required in order to monitor consolidation implications under ASC 810.

The FDIC's involvement with VIEs, in its corporate capacity, is fully described in Note 8.

RELATED PARTIES

The nature of related parties and a description of related party transactions are discussed in Note 1 and disclosed throughout the financial statements and footnotes.

DISCLOSURE ABOUT RECENT RELEVANT ACCOUNTING PRONOUNCEMENTS

Recent accounting pronouncements have been deemed to be not applicable or material to the financial statements as presented.

4

DIF

3. Investment in U.S. Treasury Obligations, Net

As of December 31, 2012 and 2011, investments in U.S. Treasury obligations, net, were $34.9 billion and $33.9 billion, respectively. As of December 31, 2012 and 2011, the DIF held $5.3 billion and $5.0 billion, respectively, of Treasury Inflation Protected Securities (TIPS), which are indexed to increases or decreases in the Consumer Price Index for All Urban Consumers (CPI U). During 2012, the FDIC sold securities designated as available for sale for total proceeds of $2.6 billion. The gross realized gains and losses on these sales were $878 thousand and $241 thousand, respectively, which resulted in a total net gain of $637 thousand. The cost of these securities sold was determined based on specific identification. Since these securities were purchased on behalf of the TLGP, the realized gain was recognized in the "Deferred revenue systemic risk" line item on the Balance Sheet.

Total Investment in U.S. Treasury Obligations, Net at December 31, 2012
DOLLARS IN THOUSANDS

Maturity	Yield at Purchase (a)	Face Value	Net Carrying Amount	Unrealized Holding Gains	Unrealized Holding Losses	Fair Value
U.S. Treasury notes and bonds						
Within 1 year	0.34%	$ 24,800,000	$ 25,228,393	$ 19,871	$ 0	$ 25,248,264
After 1 year through 5 years	0.32%	4,050,000	4,341,814	4,569	0	4,346,383
U.S. Treasury Inflation-Protected Securities						
Within 1 year	-0.86%	1,650,000	1,813,291	0	(9,788) (b)	1,803,503
After 1 year through 5 years	-0.87%	2,900,000	3,451,371	19,167	0	3,470,538
Total		$ 33,400,000	$ 34,834,869	$ 43,607	$ (9,788)	$ 34,868,688

(a) For TIPS, the yields in the above table are stated at their real yields at purchase, not their effective yields. Effective yields on TIPS include a long-term annual inflation assumption as measured by the CPI-U. The long-term CPI-U consensus forecast is 2.0 percent, based on figures issued by the Congressional Budget Office and *Blue Chip Economic Indicators* in early 2012.

(b) The unrealized losses occurred as a result of temporary changes in market interest rates. These unrealized losses occurred over a period of less than a year. The FDIC does not intend to sell the TIPS and is not likely to be required to sell them before their maturity in 2013, thus, the FDIC does not consider these securities to be other than temporarily impaired at December 31, 2012.

5

DIF

Total Investment in U.S. Treasury Obligations, Net at December 31, 2011
DOLLARS IN THOUSANDS

Maturity	Yield at Purchase (a)	Face Value		Net Carrying Amount	Unrealized Holding Gains	Unrealized Holding Losses	Fair Value
U.S. Treasury notes and bonds							
Within 1 year	0.27%	$ 24,500,000	(b) $	24,889,547	$ 17,842	$ (93)	$ 24,907,296
After 1 year through 5 years	0.93%	3,900,000		3,923,428	38,778	0	3,962,206
U.S. Treasury Inflation-Protected Securities							
Within 1 year	0.51%	1,200,000		1,537,664	659	(8)	1,538,315
After 1 year through 5 years	-0.92%	3,050,000		3,464,909	0	(9,481)	3,455,428
Total		$ 32,650,000		$ 33,815,548	$ 57,279	$ (9,582) (c)	$ 33,863,245

(a) For TIPS, the yields in the above table are stated at their real yields at purchase, not their effective yields. Effective yields on TIPS include a long-term annual inflation assumption as measured by the CPI-U. The long-term CPI-U consensus forecast is 1.8 percent, based on figures issued by the Congressional Budget Office and *Blue Chip Economic Indicators* in early 2011.

(b) Includes one Treasury note totaling $1.8 billion which matured on Saturday, December 31, 2011. Settlement occurred on the next business day, January 3, 2012.

(c) All unrealized losses occurred as a result of temporary changes in market interest rates. These unrealized losses occurred over a period of less than a year. Unrealized losses related to the TIPS converted to unrealized gains by January 31, 2012, and unrealized losses related to the U.S. Treasury notes and bonds existed on just one security that matured with no unrealized loss on January 31, 2012, and thus the FDIC does not consider these securities to be other than temporarily impaired at December 31, 2011.

4. Receivables from Resolutions, Net

Receivables from Resolutions, Net at December 31
DOLLARS IN THOUSANDS

	2012	2011
Receivables from closed banks	$ 116,940,999	$ 121,369,428
Allowance for losses	(93,821,445)	(92,821,032)
Total	$ 23,119,554	$ 28,548,396

The receivables from resolutions result from payments made by the DIF to cover obligations to insured depositors (subrogated claims), advances to resolution entities for working capital, and administrative expenses paid on behalf of resolution entities. Any related allowance for loss represents the difference between the funds advanced and/or obligations incurred and the expected repayment. Estimated future payments on losses incurred on assets sold to an acquiring institution under a shared loss agreement (SLA) are factored into the computation of the expected repayment. Assets held by DIF resolution entities (including structured transaction related assets; see Note 8) are the main source of repayment of the DIF's receivables from resolutions.

As of December 31, 2012, there were 463 active receiverships, including 51 established in 2012. As of December 31, 2012 and 2011, DIF resolution entities held assets with a book value of $53.5 billion and $71.4 billion, respectively (including $36.5 billion and $50.5 billion, respectively, of cash, investments, receivables due from the DIF, and other receivables). Ninety

6

DIF

nine percent of the current asset book value of $53.5 billion is held by resolution entities established since the beginning of 2008.

Estimated cash recoveries from the management and disposition of assets that are used to determine the allowance for losses are based on asset recovery rates from several sources including actual or pending institution specific asset disposition data, failed institution specific asset valuation data, aggregate asset valuation data on several recently failed or troubled institutions, sampled asset valuation data, and empirical asset recovery data based on failures as far back as 1990. Methodologies for determining the asset recovery rates incorporate estimating future cash recoveries, net of applicable liquidation cost estimates, and discounting based on market based risk factors applicable to a given asset's type and quality. The resulting estimated cash recoveries are then used to derive the allowance for loss on the receivables from these resolutions.

For failed institutions resolved using a whole bank purchase and assumption transaction with an accompanying SLA, the projected future shared loss payments and recoveries on the covered assets sold to the acquiring institution under the agreement are considered in determining the allowance for loss on the receivables from these resolutions. The shared loss cost projections are based on the covered assets' intrinsic value which is determined using financial models that consider the quality, condition and type of covered assets, current and future market conditions, risk factors and estimated asset holding periods. For year end 2012 financial reporting, the shared loss cost estimates were updated for the majority (93% or 276) of the 298 active shared loss agreements; the remaining 22 were based on recent loss estimates. The updated shared loss cost projections for the larger agreements were primarily based on new third party valuations estimating the cumulative loss of covered assets. The remaining agreements were stratified by receivership age. A random sample of institutions within each age stratum was selected for new third party loss estimations, and valuation results from the sample institutions were aggregated and extrapolated to institutions within the like age stratum based on asset type and performance status.

Note that estimated asset recoveries are regularly evaluated during the year, but remain subject to uncertainties because of potential changes in economic and market conditions. Continuing economic uncertainties could cause the DIF's actual recoveries to vary significantly from current estimates.

WHOLE BANK PURCHASE AND ASSUMPTION TRANSACTIONS WITH SHARED-LOSS AGREEMENTS

Since the beginning of 2008, the FDIC resolved 301 failures using whole bank purchase and assumption resolution transactions with accompanying SLAs on total assets of $214.6 billion purchased by the financial institution acquirers. The acquirer typically assumes all of the deposits and purchases essentially all of the assets of a failed institution. The majority of the commercial and residential loan assets are purchased under an SLA, where the FDIC agrees to share in future losses and recoveries experienced by the acquirer on those assets covered under the agreement. SLAs are used by the FDIC to keep assets in the private sector and to minimize disruptions to loan customers.

7

DIF

Losses on the covered assets are shared between the acquirer and the FDIC in its receivership capacity of the failed institution when losses occur through the sale, foreclosure, loan modification, or write down of loans in accordance with the terms of the SLA. The majority of the agreements cover a five to 10 year period with the receiver covering 80 percent of the losses incurred by the acquirer and the acquiring bank covering 20 percent. Prior to March 26, 2010, most SLAs included a threshold amount, above which the receiver covered 95 percent of the losses incurred by the acquirer. As mentioned above, the estimated shared loss liability is accounted for by the receiver and is included in the calculation of the DIF's allowance for loss against the corporate receivable from the resolution. As shared loss claims are asserted and proven, DIF receiverships satisfy these shared loss payments using available liquidation funds and/or by drawing on amounts due from the DIF for funding the deposits assumed by the acquirer (see Note 7).

As of December 31, 2012, 286 receiverships have made shared loss payments totaling $23.3 billion. In addition, DIF receiverships are estimated to pay an additional $18.1 billion over the duration of these SLAs on $103.7 billion in total remaining covered assets.

CONCENTRATION OF CREDIT RISK

Financial instruments that potentially subject the DIF to concentrations of credit risk are receivables from resolutions. The repayment of the DIF's receivables from resolutions is primarily influenced by recoveries on assets held by DIF receiverships and payments on the covered assets under SLAs. The majority of the $120.7 billion in remaining assets in liquidation ($17.0 billion) and current shared loss covered assets ($103.7 billion) are concentrated in commercial loans ($60.0 billion), residential loans ($43.6 billion), securities ($3.1 billion), and structured transaction related assets as described in Note 8 ($12.1 billion). Most of the assets in these asset types originated from failed institutions located in California ($34.3 billion), Florida ($14.1 billion), Puerto Rico ($10.9 billion), Illinois ($10.5 billion), Georgia ($9.8 billion) and Alabama ($9.0 billion).

5. Trust Preferred Securities

Pursuant to a systemic risk determination, the Treasury, the FDIC, and the Federal Reserve Bank of New York executed terms of a guarantee agreement on January 15, 2009 with Citigroup to provide loss protection on a pool of approximately $301.0 billion of assets that remained on the balance sheet of Citigroup. In consideration for its portion of the shared loss guarantee at inception, the FDIC received $3.025 billion of Citigroup's preferred stock. All shares of the preferred stock were subsequently converted to Citigroup Capital XXXIII trust preferred securities (TruPs) with a liquidation amount of $1,000 per security and a distribution rate of 8 percent per annum payable quarterly. The principal amount is due in 2039.

On December 23, 2009, Citigroup terminated the guarantee agreement, citing improvements in its financial condition. The FDIC incurred no loss from the guarantee prior to the termination of the agreement. In connection with the early termination of the agreement, the FDIC agreed to reduce its portion of the $3.025 billion in TruPs by $800 million. However, pursuant to an agreement between the Treasury and the FDIC, the Treasury agreed to return $800 million in

8

DIF

TruPs on behalf of the FDIC from its portion of Citigroup TruPs holdings received as a result of the shared loss agreement. The FDIC retained the $800 million of Citigroup TruPs as security in the event payments were required to be made by the DIF for guaranteed debt instruments issued by Citigroup and its affiliates under the TLGP. Because no payments were required prior to expiration of the TLGP on December 31, 2012, the FDIC transferred the $800 million in Citigroup TruPs and $183 million in related dividends and interest to the Treasury.

The remaining $2.225 billion (liquidation amount) of TruPs is classified as available for sale debt securities in accordance with FASB ASC Topic 320, *Investments   Debt and Equity Securities*. At December 31, 2012, the fair value of the TruPs was $2.264 billion (see Note 15). An unrealized holding gain of $302 million is included in accumulated other comprehensive income.

6. Property and Equipment, Net

Property and Equipment, Net at December 31
DOLLARS IN THOUSANDS

	2012	2011
Land	$ 37,352	$ 37,352
Buildings (including leasehold improvements)	313,221	316,129
Application software (includes work-in-process)	135,059	130,718
Furniture, fixtures, and equipment	152,280	159,120
Accumulated depreciation	(245,032)	(241,404)
Total	**$ 392,880**	**$ 401,915**

The depreciation expense was $76 million and $78 million for 2012 and 2011, respectively.

7. Liabilities Due to Resolutions

As of December 31, 2012 and 2011, the DIF recorded liabilities totaling $21.1 billion and $32.7 billion, respectively, to resolution entities representing the agreed upon value of assets transferred from the receiverships, at the time of failure, to the acquirers/bridge institutions for use in funding the deposits assumed by the acquirers/bridge institutions. Ninety one percent of these liabilities are due to failures resolved under whole bank purchase and assumption transactions, most with an accompanying SLA. The DIF satisfies these liabilities either by directly sending cash to the receivership to fund shared loss and other expenses or by offsetting receivables from resolutions when the receivership declares a dividend.

In addition, there was $56 million and $80 million in unpaid deposit claims related to multiple receiverships as of December 31, 2012 and 2011, respectively. The DIF pays these liabilities when the claims are approved.

9

DIF

8. Contingent Liabilities for:

ANTICIPATED FAILURE OF INSURED INSTITUTIONS

The DIF records a contingent liability and a loss provision for DIF insured institutions that are likely to fail, absent some favorable event such as obtaining additional capital or merging, when the liability is probable and reasonably estimable. The contingent liability is derived by applying expected failure rates and loss rates to the institutions based on supervisory ratings, balance sheet characteristics, and projected capital levels.

Banking industry performance continued to recover in 2012 at a gradual, steady pace. According to the quarterly financial data submitted by IDIs, the industry reported total net income of $107.4 billion for the first three quarters of 2012, an increase of 14.9% over the first three quarters of 2011. Improving credit performance, which has led to lower loan loss provisions, has been primarily responsible for most of the improvement in earnings. Losses to the DIF from failures that occurred in 2012 fell short of the amount reserved at the end of 2011, as the aggregate number and size of institution failures in 2012 were less than anticipated. The removal from the reserve of institutions that did fail in 2012, as well as projected favorable trends in bank supervisory downgrade and failure rates, all contributed to a decline by $3.3 billion to $3.2 billion in the contingent liability for anticipated failures of insured institutions at December 31, 2012.

In addition to these recorded contingent liabilities, the FDIC has identified risk in the financial services industry that could result in additional losses to the DIF should potentially vulnerable insured institutions ultimately fail. As a result of these risks, the FDIC believes that it is reasonably possible that the DIF could incur additional estimated losses of up to $6.3 billion for year end 2012 as compared to $10.2 billion for year end 2011. The actual losses, if any, will largely depend on future economic and market conditions and could differ materially from this estimate.

During 2012, 51 institutions failed with combined assets at the date of failure of $11.8 billion. Supervisory and market data suggest that the financial performance of the banking industry should continue to improve over the coming year. However, ongoing asset quality problems and limited opportunities for earnings growth will continue to be sources of stress on the industry. In addition, two key risks continue to weigh on the economic outlook. First, uncertain prospects for the European economy have increased volatility in the global financial markets, which could trigger increased volatility in the U.S. financial markets and adversely affect the U.S. economy. Second, the outcome of continued negotiations on the federal debt limit and the federal budget in 2013 could significantly affect the U.S. economy and, in turn, IDIs. The FDIC continues to evaluate the ongoing risks to affected institutions in light of existing economic and financial conditions, and the extent to which such risks will continue to put stress on the resources of the insurance fund.

LITIGATION LOSSES

The DIF records an estimated loss for unresolved legal cases to the extent that those losses are considered probable and reasonably estimable. The FDIC recorded probable litigation losses of $8 million and $1 million for the DIF as of December 31, 2012 and 2011, respectively, and has

10

DIF

determined that there are no reasonably possible losses from unresolved cases.

OTHER CONTINGENCIES
IndyMac Federal Bank Representation and Indemnification Contingent Liability
On March 19, 2009, the FDIC as receiver of IndyMac Federal Bank (IMFB) and certain subsidiaries (collectively, sellers) sold substantially all of the assets of IMFB and the respective subsidiaries, including mortgage loans and mortgage loan servicing rights, to OneWest Bank and its affiliates. To maximize sale returns, the sellers made certain representations customarily made by commercial parties regarding the assets and agreed to indemnify the acquirers for losses incurred as a result of breaches of such representations, losses incurred as a result of the failure to obtain contractual counterparty consents to the sale, and third party claims arising from pre sale acts and omissions of the sellers or the failed bank. Although the representations and indemnifications were made by or are obligations of the sellers, the FDIC, in its corporate capacity, guaranteed the receivership's indemnification obligations under the sale agreements. The representations relate generally to ownership of and right to sell the assets; compliance with applicable law in the origination of the loans; accuracy of the servicing records; validity of loan documents; and servicing of the loans serviced for others. Until the periods for asserting claims under these arrangements have expired and all indemnification claims quantified and paid, losses could continue to be incurred by the receivership and, in turn, the DIF, either directly, as a result of the FDIC corporate guaranty of the receivership's indemnification obligations, or indirectly, as a result of a reduction in the receivership's assets available to pay the DIF's claims as subrogee for insured accountholders. The acquirers' rights to assert claims to recover losses incurred as a result of breaches of loan seller representations extend out to March 19, 2019 for the Fannie Mae and Ginnie Mae reverse mortgage servicing portfolios (unpaid principal balance of $16.2 billion at December 31, 2012 compared to $16.7 billion at December 31, 2011), and March 19, 2014 for the Fannie Mae, Freddie Mac and Ginnie Mae mortgage servicing portfolios (unpaid principal balance of $34.3 billion at December 31, 2012 compared to $38.5 billion at December 31, 2011). The acquirers' rights to assert claims to recover losses incurred as a result of other third party claims (including due to pre March 19, 2009 acts or omissions) and breaches of servicer representations, including liability with respect to the Fannie Mae, Ginnie Mae and Freddie Mac portfolios as well as the private mortgage servicing portfolio and whole loans (unpaid principal balance of $53.9 billion at December 31, 2012 compared to $62.0 billion at December 31, 2011) expired on March 19, 2011. As of the expiration date of this claim period, notices relating to potential defects were received, but they require review to determine whether a valid defect exists and, if so, the identification and costing of possible cure actions. It is highly unlikely that all of these potential defects will result in losses.

The IndyMac receivership has paid a cumulative total of $14 million in approved claims through December 31, 2012 and a cumulative total of $5 million through December 31, 2011. Additional claims asserted, but under review, were accrued in the amount of $1 million as of December 31, 2012 and $2 million as of December 31, 2011. Alleged breaches of origination and servicing representations exist, and it is probable that the IndyMac receivership and its subsidiary Financial Freedom Senior Funding Corporation may incur up to $80 million in losses; these estimated losses have been accrued as of December 31, 2012. In addition, review and evaluation is in process for approximately $32 million in reasonably possible liabilities with respect to alleged breaches of representations and warranties. Potential losses relating to origination and

11

servicing representations, which currently cannot be quantified, may also be incurred under other agreements with investors.

The FDIC believes it is likely that additional losses will be incurred, however quantifying the contingent liability associated with the representations and the indemnification obligations is subject to a number of uncertainties, including (1) borrower prepayment speeds, (2) the occurrence of borrower defaults and resulting foreclosures and losses, (3) the assertion by third party investors of claims with respect to loans serviced for them, (4) the existence and timing of discovery of breaches and the assertion of claims for indemnification for losses by the acquirer, (5) the compliance by the acquirer with certain loss mitigation and other conditions to indemnification, (6) third party sources of loss recovery (such as title companies and insurers), (7) the ability of the acquirer to refute claims from investors without incurring reimbursable losses, and (8) the cost to cure breaches and respond to third party claims. The difficulty in assessing losses is exacerbated further by the inability to use historical default and loss rates as a metric given recent economic events. Because of these and other uncertainties that surround the liability associated with indemnifications and the quantification of possible losses, the FDIC has determined that while additional losses are probable, the amount is not estimable.

Purchase and Assumption Indemnification

In connection with purchase and assumption agreements for resolutions, the FDIC in its receivership capacity generally indemnifies the purchaser of a failed institution's assets and liabilities in the event a third party asserts a claim against the purchaser unrelated to the explicit assets purchased or liabilities assumed at the time of failure. The FDIC in its corporate capacity is a secondary guarantor if a receivership is unable to pay. These indemnifications generally extend for a term of six years after the date of institution failure. The FDIC is unable to estimate the maximum potential liability for these types of guarantees as the agreements do not specify a maximum amount and any payments are dependent upon the outcome of future contingent events, the nature and likelihood of which cannot be determined at this time. During 2012 and 2011, the FDIC in its corporate capacity made no indemnification payments under such agreements, and no amount has been accrued in the accompanying financial statements with respect to these indemnification guarantees.

FDIC Guaranteed Debt of Structured Transactions

The FDIC as receiver uses three types of structured transactions to dispose of certain performing and non performing residential mortgage loans, commercial loans, construction loans, and mortgage backed securities held by the receiverships. The three types of structured transactions are 1) limited liability companies (LLCs), 2) securitizations, and 3) structured sale of guaranteed notes (SSGNs).

LLCs

Under the LLC structure, the FDIC in its receivership capacity contributes a pool of assets to a newly formed LLC and offers for sale, through a competitive bid process, some of the equity in the LLC. The day to day management of the LLC transfers to the highest bidder along with the purchased equity interest. In many instances, the FDIC in its corporate capacity guarantees notes issued by the LLCs. In exchange for a guarantee, the DIF receives a guarantee fee in either 1) a lump sum, up front payment based on the estimated duration of the note or 2) a monthly payment based on a fixed percentage multiplied by the outstanding note balance. The terms of

12

DIF

these guarantee agreements generally stipulate that all cash flows received from the entity's collateral be used to pay, in the following order, 1) operational expenses of the entity, 2) the FDIC's contractual guarantee fee, 3) the guaranteed notes (or, if applicable, fund the related defeasance account for payoff of the notes at maturity), and 4) the equity investors. If the FDIC is required to perform under these guarantees, it acquires an interest in the cash flows of the LLC equal to the amount of guarantee payments made plus accrued interest thereon. Once all expenses have been paid, the guaranteed notes have been satisfied, and the FDIC has been reimbursed for any guarantee payments, the equity holders receive any remaining cash flows.

Since 2009, private investors have purchased a 40 to 50 percent ownership interest in the LLC structures for $1.6 billion in cash and the LLCs issued notes of $4.4 billion to the receiverships to partially fund the purchase of the assets. The receiverships hold the remaining 50 to 60 percent equity interest in the LLCs and, in most cases, the guaranteed notes. The FDIC in its corporate capacity guarantees the timely payment of principal and interest due on the notes. The terms of the note guarantees extend until the earlier of 1) payment in full of the notes or 2) two years following the maturity date of the notes. The note with the longest term matures in 2020. In the event of note payment default, the FDIC as guarantor is entitled to exercise or cause the exercise of certain rights and remedies including: 1) accelerating the payment of the unpaid principal amount of the notes; 2) selling the assets held as collateral; or 3) foreclosing on the equity interests of the debtor.

Securitizations and SSGNs
Securitizations and SSGNs (collectively, "trusts") are transactions in which certain assets or securities from failed institutions are pooled and transferred into a trust structure. The trusts issue 1) senior and/or subordinated debt instruments and 2) owner trust or residual certificates collateralized by the underlying mortgage backed securities or loans.

Since 2010, private investors purchased the senior notes issued by the trusts for $5.7 billion in cash. The receiverships hold 100 percent of the subordinated debt instruments and owner trust or residual certificates. The FDIC in its corporate capacity guarantees the timely payment of principal and interest due on the senior notes, the latest maturity of which is 2050. In exchange for the guarantee, the DIF receives a monthly payment based on a fixed percentage multiplied by the outstanding note balance. These guarantee agreements generally stipulate that all cash flows received from the entity's collateral be used to pay, in the following order, 1) operational expenses of the entity, 2) the FDIC's contractual guarantee fee, 3) interest on the guaranteed notes, 4) principal of the guaranteed notes, and 5) the holders of the subordinated notes and owner trust or residual certificates. If the FDIC is required to perform under its guarantees, it acquires an interest in the cash flows of the trust equal to the amount of guarantee payments made plus accrued interest thereon. Once all expenses have been paid, the guaranteed notes have been satisfied, and the FDIC has been reimbursed for any guarantee payments, the subordinated note holders and owner trust or residual certificates holders receive the remaining cash flows.

All Structured Transactions with FDIC Guaranteed Debt
Through December 31, 2012, the receiverships have transferred a portfolio of loans with an unpaid principal balance of $16.4 billion and mortgage backed securities with a book value of $8.1 billion to 14 LLCs and 9 trusts. The LLCs and trusts subsequently issued notes guaranteed by the FDIC in an original principal amount of $10.1 billion. As of December 31, 2012 and

13

DIF

2011, the DIF collected guarantee fees totaling $218 million and $203 million, respectively, and recorded a receivable for additional guarantee fees of $95 million and $106 million, respectively, included in the "Interest receivable on investments and other assets, net" line item on the Balance Sheet. All guarantee fees are recorded as deferred revenue, included in the "Accounts payable and other liabilities" line item, and recognized as revenue primarily on a straight line basis over the term of the notes. At December 31, 2012 and 2011, the amount of deferred revenue recorded was $101 million and $134 million, respectively. The DIF records no other structured transaction related assets or liabilities on its balance sheet.

The estimated loss to the DIF from the guarantees is derived from an analysis of the net present value (using a discount rate of 3 percent) of the expected guarantee payments by the FDIC, reimbursements to the FDIC for guarantee payments, and guarantee fee collections. The FDIC believes that it is reasonably possible that the DIF could incur an estimated loss for one transaction of $5.7 million in 2020, net of expected guarantee fees of $4.2 million. This estimated loss may vary over time as conditions change. For all of the remaining transactions, the cash flows from the LLC or trust assets provide sufficient coverage to fully pay the debts. To date, the FDIC in its corporate capacity has not provided, and does not intend to provide, any form of financial or other type of support to a trust or LLC that it was not previously contractually required to provide.

As of December 31, 2012 and 2011, the maximum loss exposure was $2.2 billion and $3.7 billion for LLCs and $3.2 billion and $3.9 billion for trusts, respectively, representing the sum of all outstanding debt guaranteed by the FDIC in its corporate capacity. Some transactions have established defeasance accounts to pay off the notes at maturity. As of December 31, 2012 and 2011, a total of $1.6 billion and $2.2 billion, respectively, has been deposited into these accounts.

9. Assessments

The Dodd Frank Act provided for significant assessment and capitalization reforms for the DIF. In response, the FDIC implemented several changes to the assessment system and developed a comprehensive, long term fund management plan. The plan is designed to restore and maintain a positive fund balance for the DIF even during a banking crisis and achieve moderate, steady assessment rates throughout any economic cycle. Summarized below are actions taken to implement assessment system changes and provisions of the comprehensive plan.

RESTORATION PLAN
In October 2010, the FDIC adopted a Restoration Plan to ensure that the ratio of the DIF fund balance to estimated insured deposits (reserve ratio) reaches 1.35 percent by September 30, 2020 in lieu of the previous target of 1.15 percent by the end of 2016. In addition, the Plan provides for the FDIC to 1) pursue rulemaking regarding the method that will be used to offset the impact of the increased reserve ratio on small institutions (less than $10 billion in assets) and 2) update, at least semiannually, its loss and income projections for the fund and, if needed, increase or decrease assessment rates, following notice and comment rulemaking, if required.

14

DIF

DESIGNATED RESERVE RATIO
In December 2012, the FDIC adopted a final rule maintaining the designated reserve ratio (DRR) at 2 percent, effective January 1, 2013. The DRR is an integral part of the FDIC's comprehensive, long term management plan for the DIF and is viewed as a long range, minimum target for the reserve ratio.

CALCULATION OF ASSESSMENT
In February 2011, the FDIC adopted a final rule, effective on April 1, 2011, amending part 327 of title 12 of the Code of Federal Regulations to 1) redefine the assessment base used for calculating deposit insurance assessments from adjusted domestic deposits to average consolidated total assets minus average tangible equity (measured as Tier 1 capital); 2) change the assessment rate adjustments; 3) lower the initial base rate schedule and the total base rate schedule for all IDIs to collect approximately the same revenue for the DIF as would have been collected under the old assessment base; 4) suspend dividends indefinitely, and, in lieu of dividends, adopt lower assessment rate schedules when the reserve ratio reaches 1.15 percent, 2 percent, and 2.5 percent; and 5) change the risk based assessment system for large IDIs (generally, those institutions with at least $10 billion in total assets). Specifically, the final rule eliminates risk categories and the use of long term debt issuer ratings for large institutions and combines CAMELS ratings and certain forward looking financial measures into two scorecards: one for most large institutions and another for large institutions that are structurally and operationally complex or that pose unique challenges and risks in case of failure (highly complex IDIs).

In October 2012, the FDIC adopted a final rule which amends and clarifies some definitions of higher risk assets as used in the deposit insurance pricing scorecards for large and highly complex IDIs by 1) revising the definitions of certain higher risk assets, specifically leveraged loans and subprime consumer loans, 2) clarifying when an asset must be identified as higher risk, and 3) clarifying the way securitizations are identified as higher risk. The goal of this final rule is to ensure that the assessment system captures the risk inherent in higher risk assets without imposing an unnecessary reporting burden. The final rule will become effective on April 1, 2013 and provides that, until then, large and highly complex IDIs will continue to report higher risk assets using existing guidance.

ASSESSMENT REVENUE
Annual assessment rates averaged approximately 10.1 cents per $100 and 11.1 cents per $100 of the new assessment base (as described above) for all of 2012 and the last three quarters of 2011, respectively. The annual assessment rate averaged approximately 17.6 cents per $100 of the adjusted domestic deposits assessment base for the first quarter of 2011.

In December 2009, a majority of IDIs prepaid $45.7 billion of estimated quarterly risk based assessments to address the DIF's liquidity need to pay for projected failures and to ensure that the deposit insurance system remained industry funded. For the fourth quarter 2009 and each subsequent quarter, an institution's risk based deposit insurance assessment was offset by the available amount of prepaid assessments, thereby reducing that institution's prepaid assessment balance. By regulation, any remaining prepaid assessments must be refunded to the institutions after collection of the amount due on June 30, 2013. The final prepaid offset will occur in June 2013 for the assessment period ending March 31, 2013. Therefore, at December 31, 2012, the

15

DIF

"Unearned revenue prepaid assessments" line item on the Balance Sheet of $1.6 billion
represents the final estimated prepaid offset and the "Refunds of prepaid assessments" line item
reflects the estimate of $5.7 billion that will be returned to the institutions in June 2013. Though
the combined total for both the prepaid offset and refunds will remain unchanged, the estimated
amount for each component may vary considerably because of the uncertainty inherent in
projecting the assessment rate and base for IDIs beyond the customary 90 day period.

For those institutions that did not prepay assessments or whose prepaid assessments have been
exhausted, the "Assessments receivable, net" line item on the Balance Sheet of $1.0 billion and
$282 million as of December 31, 2012 and 2011, respectively, represents the estimated
premiums due from IDIs for the fourth quarter of 2012 and 2011, respectively.

RESERVE RATIO
As of September 30, 2012, the DIF reserve ratio was 0.35 percent of estimated insured deposits.

ASSESSMENTS RELATED TO FICO
Assessments continue to be levied on institutions for payments of the interest on obligations
issued by the Financing Corporation (FICO). The FICO was established as a mixed ownership
government corporation to function solely as a financing vehicle for the former FSLIC. The
annual FICO interest obligation of approximately $790 million is paid on a pro rata basis using
the same rate for banks and thrifts. The FICO assessment has no financial impact on the DIF and
is separate from deposit insurance assessments. The FDIC, as administrator of the DIF, acts
solely as a collection agent for the FICO. During 2012 and 2011, approximately $797 million
and $795 million, respectively, was collected and remitted to the FICO.

10. Other Revenue

Other Revenue for the Years Ended December 31
DOLLARS IN THOUSANDS

		2012		2011
Temporary Liquidity Guarantee Program revenue (Note 16)	$	5,885,330	$	2,569,579
Dividends and interest on Citigroup trust preferred securities (Note 5)		177,831		178,000
Guarantee fees for structured transactions (Note 8)		57,206		92,229
Other		6,844		7,121
Total	$	6,127,211	$	2,846,929

TEMPORARY LIQUIDITY GUARANTEE PROGRAM REVENUE
Pursuant to a systemic risk determination in October 2008, the FDIC established the TLGP (see
Note 16). In exchange for guarantees issued under the TLGP, the DIF received fees that were set
aside, as deferred revenue, for potential TLGP losses. As losses occurred, the DIF recognized
the losses as systemic risk expenses and offset the losses by recognizing an equivalent portion of
the deferred revenue as systemic risk revenue. This accounting practice isolated systemic risk
activities from the normal operating activities of the DIF.

16

DIF

In accordance with FDIC policy, the DIF recognized revenue during the guarantee period when guarantee fees held were determined to be in excess of amounts needed to cover potential losses, and, for all remaining TLGP assets held as deferred revenue, upon expiration of the TLGP on December 31, 2012. As a result, the DIF recognized total revenue of $5.9 billion and $2.6 billion in 2012 and 2011, respectively.

11. Operating Expenses

Operating expenses were $1.8 billion and $1.6 billion for 2012 and 2011, respectively. The chart below lists the major components of operating expenses.

Operating Expenses for the Years Ended December 31
DOLLARS IN THOUSANDS

	2012	2011
Salaries and benefits	$ 1,300,697	$ 1,320,991
Outside services	337,379	342,502
Travel	106,897	115,135
Buildings and leased space	91,631	93,630
Software/Hardware maintenance	63,108	58,981
Depreciation of property and equipment	76,365	77,720
Other	21,137	46,652
Subtotal	1,997,214	2,055,611
Services billed to resolution entities	(219,701)	(430,260)
Total	$ 1,777,513	$ 1,625,351

12. Provision for Insurance Losses

Provision for insurance losses was negative $4.2 billion for 2012, compared to negative $4.4 billion for 2011. The negative provision for 2012 primarily resulted from a reduction of $1.4 billion in the contingent loss reserve due to the improvement in the financial condition of institutions that were previously identified to fail and a decrease of $2.8 billion in the estimated losses for institutions that failed in the current and prior years.

13. Employee Benefits

PENSION BENEFITS AND SAVINGS PLANS
Eligible FDIC employees (permanent and term employees with appointments exceeding one year) are covered by the federal government retirement plans, either the Civil Service Retirement System (CSRS) or the Federal Employees Retirement System (FERS). Although the DIF contributes a portion of pension benefits for eligible employees, it does not account for the assets of either retirement system. The DIF also does not have actuarial data for accumulated plan

17

DIF

benefits or the unfunded liability relative to eligible employees. These amounts are reported on and accounted for by the U.S. Office of Personnel Management (OPM).

Eligible FDIC employees also may participate in a FDIC sponsored tax deferred 401(k) savings plan with matching contributions up to 5 percent. Under the Federal Thrift Savings Plan (TSP), the FDIC provides FERS employees with an automatic contribution of 1 percent of pay and an additional matching contribution up to 4 percent of pay. CSRS employees also can contribute to the TSP, but they do not receive agency matching contributions.

Pension Benefits and Savings Plans Expenses for the Years Ended December 31

DOLLARS IN THOUSANDS

	2012	2011
Civil Service Retirement System	$ 5,960	$ 6,140
Federal Employees Retirement System (Basic Benefit)	97,517	95,846
FDIC Savings Plan	37,700	36,645
Federal Thrift Savings Plan	34,555	33,910
Total	$ 175,732	$ 172,541

POSTRETIREMENT BENEFITS OTHER THAN PENSIONS

The DIF has no postretirement health insurance liability since all eligible retirees are covered by the Federal Employees Health Benefits (FEHB) program. The FEHB is administered and accounted for by the OPM. In addition, OPM pays the employer share of the retiree's health insurance premiums.

The FDIC provides certain life and dental insurance coverage for its eligible retirees, the retirees' beneficiaries, and covered dependents. Retirees eligible for life and dental insurance coverage are those who have qualified due to 1) immediate enrollment upon appointment or five years of participation in the plan and 2) eligibility for an immediate annuity. The life insurance program provides basic coverage at no cost to retirees and allows converting optional coverage to direct pay plans. For the dental coverage, retirees are responsible for a portion of the dental premium.

The FDIC has elected not to fund the postretirement life and dental benefit liabilities. As a result, the DIF recognized the underfunded status (the difference between the accumulated postretirement benefit obligation and the plan assets at fair value) as a liability. Since there are no plan assets, the plan's benefit liability is equal to the accumulated postretirement benefit obligation. At December 31, 2012 and 2011, the liability was $224 million and $188 million, respectively, which is recognized in the "Postretirement benefit liability" line item on the Balance Sheet. The cumulative actuarial losses (changes in assumptions and plan experience) and prior service costs (changes to plan provisions that increase benefits) were $60 million and $34 million at December 31, 2012 and 2011, respectively. These amounts are reported as accumulated other comprehensive income in the "Unrealized postretirement benefit loss" line item on the Balance Sheet.

The DIF's expenses for postretirement benefits for 2012 and 2011 were $14 million and $12 million, respectively, which are included in the current and prior year's operating expenses on the Statement of Income and Fund Balance. The changes in the actuarial losses and prior service costs for 2012 and 2011 of $27 million and $15 million, respectively, are reported as other comprehensive income in the "Unrealized postretirement benefit loss" line item on the Statement

18

DIF

of Income and Fund Balance. Key actuarial assumptions used in the accounting for the plan include the discount rate of 3.75 percent, the rate of compensation increase of 4.0 percent, and the dental coverage trend rate of 5.6 percent. The discount rate of 3.75 percent is based upon rates of return on high quality fixed income investments whose cash flows match the timing and amount of expected benefit payments.

14. Commitments and Off-Balance-Sheet Exposure

COMMITMENTS:
Leased Space
The FDIC's lease commitments total $216 million for future years. The lease agreements contain escalation clauses resulting in adjustments, usually on an annual basis. The DIF recognized leased space expense of $54 million and $56 million for the years ended December 31, 2012 and 2011, respectively.

Leased Space Commitments

DOLLARS IN THOUSANDS

2013	2014	2015	2016	2017	2018/Thereafter
$52,160	$46,521	$36,496	$33,509	$29,068	$18,511

OFF-BALANCE-SHEET EXPOSURE:
Deposit Insurance
Estimates of insured deposits are derived primarily from quarterly financial data submitted by IDIs to the FDIC and represent the accounting loss that would be realized if all IDIs were to fail and the acquired assets provided no recoveries. As of September 30, 2012 and December 31, 2011, estimated insured deposits for the DIF were $7.3 trillion and $7.0 trillion, respectively, including $1.5 trillion and $1.4 trillion, respectively, of noninterest bearing transaction deposits that exceeded the basic limit of $250,000 per account. Under the Dodd Frank Act, noninterest bearing transaction deposits received unlimited deposit insurance coverage from December 31, 2010 through December 31, 2012. Upon expiration of this unlimited coverage on December 31, 2012, these deposits pose no further exposure to the DIF.

15. Disclosures about the Fair Value of Financial Instruments

Financial assets recognized and measured at fair value on a recurring basis at each reporting date include cash equivalents (Note 2), the investment in U.S. Treasury obligations (Note 3) and trust preferred securities (Note 5). The following tables present the DIF's financial assets measured at fair value as of December 31, 2012 and 2011.

19

DIF

Assets Measured at Fair Value at December 31, 2012

DOLLARS IN THOUSANDS

	Fair Value Measurements Using			
	Quoted Prices in Active Markets for Identical Assets (Level 1)	Significant Other Observable Inputs (Level 2)	Significant Unobservable Inputs (Level 3)	Total Assets at Fair Value
Assets				
Cash equivalents[1]	$ 3,091,778			$ 3,091,778
Available-for-Sale Debt Securities				
Investment in U.S. Treasury Obligations[2]	34,868,688			34,868,688
Trust preferred securities		2,263,983		2,263,983
Total Assets	$ 37,960,466	$ 2,263,983	$ 0	$ 40,224,449

(1) Cash equivalents are Special U.S. Treasury Certificates with overnight maturities valued at prevailing interest rates established by the U.S. Bureau of Public Debt.

(2) The investment in U.S. Treasury obligations is measured based on prevailing market yields for federal government entities.

In exchange for prior shared loss guarantee coverage provided to Citigroup, the FDIC and the Treasury received TruPs (see Note 5). At December 31, 2012, the fair value of the securities in the amount of $2.264 billion was classified as a Level 2 measurement based on an FDIC developed model using observable market data for traded Citigroup securities to determine the expected present value of future cash flows. Key inputs include market yields on U.S. dollar interest rate swaps and discount rates for default, call, and liquidity risks that are derived from traded Citigroup securities and modeled pricing relationships.

Assets Measured at Fair Value at December 31, 2011

DOLLARS IN THOUSANDS

	Fair Value Measurements Using			
	Quoted Prices in Active Markets for Identical Assets (Level 1)	Significant Other Observable Inputs (Level 2)	Significant Unobservable Inputs (Level 3)	Total Assets at Fair Value
Assets				
Cash equivalents[1]	$ 3,266,631			$ 3,266,631
Available-for-Sale Debt Securities				
Investment in U.S. Treasury obligations[2]	33,863,245			33,863,245
Trust preferred securities		$ 2,213,231		2,213,231
Trust preferred securities held for UST (Note 5)		795,769		795,769
Total Assets	$ 37,129,876	$ 3,009,000	$ 0	$ 40,138,876

(1) Cash equivalents are Special U.S. Treasury Certificates with overnight maturities valued at prevailing interest rates established by the U.S. Bureau of Public Debt.

(2) The investment in U.S. Treasury obligations is measured based on prevailing market yields for federal government entities.

Some of the DIF's financial assets and liabilities are not recognized at fair value but are recorded at amounts that approximate fair value due to their short maturities and/or comparability with current interest rates. Such items include interest receivable on investments, assessments receivable, other short term receivables, refunds of prepaid assessments, accounts payable, and other liabilities.

20

DIF

The net receivables from resolutions primarily include the DIF's subrogated claim arising from obligations to insured depositors. The resolution entity assets that will ultimately be used to pay the corporate subrogated claim are valued using discount rates that include consideration of market risk. These discounts ultimately affect the DIF's allowance for loss against the receivables from resolutions. Therefore, the corporate subrogated claim indirectly includes the effect of discounting and should not be viewed as being stated in terms of nominal cash flows.

Although the value of the corporate subrogated claim is influenced by valuation of resolution entity assets (see Note 4), such valuation is not equivalent to the valuation of the corporate claim. Since the corporate claim is unique, not intended for sale to the private sector, and has no established market, it is not practicable to estimate a fair value.

The FDIC believes that a sale to the private sector of the corporate claim would require indeterminate, but substantial, discounts for an interested party to profit from these assets because of credit and other risks. In addition, the timing of resolution entity payments to the DIF on the subrogated claim does not necessarily correspond with the timing of collections on resolution entity assets. Therefore, the effect of discounting used by resolution entities should not necessarily be viewed as producing an estimate of fair value for the net receivables from resolutions.

16. Systemic Risk Transactions

Pursuant to a systemic risk determination, the FDIC established the TLGP (codified in part 370 of title 12 of the Code of Federal Regulations) for IDIs, designated affiliates and certain holding companies on October 14, 2008, in an effort to counter the system wide crisis in the nation's financial sector. The DIF received fees in exchange for guarantees issued under the TLGP and set aside, as deferred revenue, all fees for potential TLGP losses. As systemic risk expenses were incurred, the DIF reduced deferred revenue and recognized an offsetting amount as systemic risk revenue. Also, DIF recognized systemic risk revenue when guarantee fees held were determined to be in excess of amounts needed to cover potential losses. As a result, systemic risk activities were isolated from the normal operating activities of the DIF.

At its inception, the TLGP consisted of two components: 1) the Transaction Account Guarantee Program (TAG) and 2) the Debt Guarantee Program (DGP). The TAG provided unlimited coverage for noninterest bearing transaction accounts held by IDIs on all deposit amounts exceeding the fully insured limit of $250,000 through December 31, 2010. During its existence, the FDIC collected TAG fees of $1.2 billion. Total subrogated claims arising from obligations to depositors with noninterest bearing transaction accounts were $8.8 billion, with estimated losses of $2.1 billion.

The DGP permitted participating entities to issue FDIC guaranteed senior unsecured debt through October 31, 2009. The FDIC's guarantee for all such debt expired no later than December 31, 2012. Through the end of the debt issuance period, the DIF collected $8.3 billion of guarantee fees and received additional fees of $1.2 billion from participating entities that elected to issue senior unsecured non guaranteed debt. During the program, guaranteed debt

21

issued totaled $618.0 billion and the FDIC paid $153 million in claims for principal and interest arising from the default of guaranteed debt obligations of six debt issuers.

The expiration of the guarantee period for the DGP on December 31, 2012 marked the conclusion of the TLGP. As established under terms of the TLGP, all excess funds were transferred to the DIF. Since inception, the DIF recognized total "Other revenue" of $8.5 billion (see Note 10). In 2012, the DIF received $5.2 billion of cash and a net receivable of $693 million included in "Receivables from resolutions, net". The net receivable represents estimated recoveries on payments under the TLGP to cover obligations. In 2011, the DIF received $2.6 billion of cash and U.S. Treasury obligations.

TLGP Summary (Inception through December 31, 2012)
DOLLARS IN THOUSANDS

Collections:			
Transaction Account Guarantee Program fees		$	1,156,332
Debt Guarantee Program fees			9,490,993
Interest earned on TLGP funds			42,293
Total TLGP Fees and Interest Earned		$	**10,689,618**
Payments:			
Transaction Account Guarantee Program claims	$	(8,769,873)	
Less: Receipts of receivership dividends		6,016,597	
Net Transaction Account Guarantee Program claims			(2,753,276)
Debt Guarantee Program claims paid			(153,127)
TLGP operating expenses			(6,707)
Total TLGP Claims and Expenses Paid		$	**(2,913,110)**
Cash Transferred to the DIF			**7,776,508**
Estimated Recovery on TAG Claims Paid			693,248
Excess TLGP Assets Transferred to the DIF		$	**8,469,756**

17. Subsequent Events

Subsequent events have been evaluated through February 14, 2013, the date the financial statements are available to be issued.

2013 FAILURES THROUGH FEBRUARY 14, 2013
Through February 14, 2013, two insured institutions failed in 2013 with total losses to the DIF estimated to be $43 million.

22

FSLIC Resolution Fund's Financial Statements

FSLIC RESOLUTION FUND (FRF)

Federal Deposit Insurance Corporation
FSLIC Resolution Fund Balance Sheet at December 31

DOLLARS IN THOUSANDS

	2012	2011
Assets		
Cash and cash equivalents	$ 3,594,007	$ 3,533,410
Receivables from thrift resolutions and other assets, net (Note 3)	5,456	65,163
Receivables from U.S. Treasury for goodwill litigation (Note 4)	356,455	356,455
Total Assets	$ 3,955,918	$ 3,955,028
Liabilities		
Accounts payable and other liabilities	$ 2,442	$ 3,544
Contingent liabilities for goodwill litigation (Note 4)	356,455	356,455
Total Liabilities	358,897	359,999
Resolution Equity (Note 5)		
Contributed capital	128,056,656	127,875,656
Accumulated deficit	(124,459,635)	(124,280,627)
Total Resolution Equity	3,597,021	3,595,029
Total Liabilities and Resolution Equity	$ 3,955,918	$ 3,955,028

The accompanying notes are an integral part of these financial statements.

Statement of Income and Accumulated Deficit

FSLIC RESOLUTION FUND (FRF)

Federal Deposit Insurance Corporation

FSLIC Resolution Fund Statement of Income and Accumulated Deficit for the Years Ended December 31

DOLLARS IN THOUSANDS

	2012	2011
Revenue		
Interest on U.S. Treasury obligations	$ 2,458	$ 1,361
Other revenue	2,549	3,257
Total Revenue	**5,007**	**4,618**
Expenses and Losses		
Operating expenses	4,165	4,660
Provision for losses	(1,408)	(8,578)
Goodwill litigation expenses (Note 4)	181,000	82,960
Recovery of tax benefits	0	(18,373)
Other expenses	258	205
Total Expenses and Losses	**184,015**	**60,874**
Net Loss	**(179,008)**	**(56,256)**
Accumulated Deficit - Beginning	**(124,280,627)**	**(124,224,371)**
Accumulated Deficit - Ending	$ **(124,459,635)**	$ **(124,280,627)**

The accompanying notes are an integral part of these financial statements.

Statement of Cash Flows

FSLIC RESOLUTION FUND (FRF)

Federal Deposit Insurance Corporation

FSLIC Resolution Fund Statement of Cash Flows for the Years Ended December 31

DOLLARS IN THOUSANDS

		2012		2011
Operating Activities				
Net Loss	$	(179,008)	$	(56,256)
Adjustments to reconcile net loss to				
net cash (used) by operating activities:				
Provision for losses		(1,408)		(8,578)
Change in Operating Assets and Liabilities:				
Decrease (Increase) in receivables from thrift resolutions and other assets		61,115		(33,177)
(Decrease) Increase in accounts payable and other liabilities		(1,102)		554
Increase in contingent liabilities for goodwill litigation		0		32,960
Net Cash (Used) by Operating Activities		**(120,403)**		**(64,497)**
Financing Activities				
Provided by:				
U.S. Treasury payments for goodwill litigation (Note 4)		181,000		50,000
Net Cash Provided by Financing Activities		**181,000**		**50,000**
Net Increase (Decrease) in Cash and Cash Equivalents		60,597		(14,497)
Cash and Cash Equivalents - Beginning		3,533,410		3,547,907
Cash and Cash Equivalents - Ending	$	3,594,007	$	3,533,410

The accompanying notes are an integral part of these financial statements.

Notes to the Financial Statements

NOTES TO THE FINANCIAL STATEMENTS

FSLIC RESOLUTION FUND
December 31, 2012 and 2011

1. Operations/Dissolution of the FSLIC Resolution Fund

OVERVIEW
The Federal Deposit Insurance Corporation (FDIC) is the independent deposit insurance agency created by Congress in 1933 to maintain stability and public confidence in the nation's banking system. Provisions that govern the operations of the FDIC are generally found in the Federal Deposit Insurance (FDI) Act, as amended (12 U.S.C. 1811, *et seq*). In carrying out the purposes of the FDI Act, the FDIC, as administrator of the Deposit Insurance Fund (DIF), insures the deposits of banks and savings associations (insured depository institutions). In cooperation with other federal and state agencies, the FDIC promotes the safety and soundness of insured depository institutions by identifying, monitoring and addressing risks to the DIF. Commercial banks, savings banks and savings associations (known as "thrifts") are supervised by either the FDIC, the Office of the Comptroller of the Currency, or the Federal Reserve Board. In addition, the FDIC, through administration of the FSLIC Resolution Fund (FRF), is responsible for the sale of remaining assets and satisfaction of liabilities associated with the former Federal Savings and Loan Insurance Corporation (FSLIC) and the former Resolution Trust Corporation (RTC). The DIF and the FRF are maintained separately by the FDIC to support their respective functions.

The U.S. Congress created the FSLIC through the enactment of the National Housing Act of 1934. The Financial Institutions Reform, Recovery, and Enforcement Act of 1989 (FIRREA) abolished the insolvent FSLIC, created the FRF, and transferred the assets and liabilities of the FSLIC to the FRF except those assets and liabilities transferred to the newly created RTC effective on August 9, 1989. Further, the FIRREA established the Resolution Funding Corporation (REFCORP) to provide part of the initial funds used by the RTC for thrift resolutions.

The RTC Completion Act of 1993 (RTC Completion Act) terminated the RTC as of December 31, 1995. All remaining assets and liabilities of the RTC were transferred to the FRF on January 1, 1996. Today, the FRF consists of two distinct pools of assets and liabilities: one composed of the assets and liabilities of the FSLIC transferred to the FRF upon the dissolution of the FSLIC (FRF FSLIC), and the other composed of the RTC assets and liabilities (FRF RTC). The assets of one pool are not available to satisfy obligations of the other.

OPERATIONS/DISSOLUTION OF THE FRF
The FRF will continue operations until all of its assets are sold or otherwise liquidated and all of its liabilities are satisfied. Any funds remaining in the FRF FSLIC will be paid to the U.S. Treasury. Any remaining funds of the FRF RTC will be distributed to the REFCORP to pay the interest on the REFCORP bonds. In addition, the FRF FSLIC has available until expended $602 million in appropriations to facilitate, if required, efforts to wind up the resolution activity of the FRF FSLIC.

1

FRF

The FDIC has conducted an extensive review and cataloging of FRF's remaining assets and liabilities. Some of the issues and items that remain open in FRF are 1) criminal restitution orders (generally have from 1 to 13 years remaining to enforce); 2) collections of settlements and judgments obtained against officers and directors and other professionals responsible for causing or contributing to thrift losses (generally have from 2 to 14 years remaining to enforce, unless the judgments are renewed, which will result in significantly longer periods for collection for some judgments); 3) a few assistance agreements entered into by the former FSLIC (FRF could continue to receive or refund overpayments of tax benefits sharing through 2014); 4) goodwill litigation (no final date for resolution has been established; see Note 4); and 5) affordable housing program monitoring (requirements can exceed 25 years). The FRF could potentially realize recoveries from tax benefits sharing of up to approximately $40 million; however, any associated recoveries are not reflected in FRF's financial statements given the significant uncertainties surrounding the ultimate outcome. The FDIC will consider returning a portion of the FRF FSLIC's remaining funds of $3.4 billion to the U.S. Treasury in 2013.

RECEIVERSHIP OPERATIONS
The FDIC is responsible for managing and disposing of the assets of failed institutions in an orderly and efficient manner. The assets held by receivership entities, and the claims against them, are accounted for separately from FRF assets and liabilities to ensure that receivership proceeds are distributed in accordance with applicable laws and regulations. Also, the income and expenses attributable to receiverships are accounted for as transactions of those receiverships. Receiverships are billed by the FDIC for services provided on their behalf.

2. Summary of Significant Accounting Policies

GENERAL
These financial statements pertain to the financial position, results of operations, and cash flows of the FRF and are presented in accordance with U.S. generally accepted accounting principles (GAAP). As permitted by the Federal Accounting Standards Advisory Board's Statement of Federal Financial Accounting Standards 34, *The Hierarchy of Generally Accepted Accounting Principles, Including the Application of Standards Issued by the Financial Accounting Standards Board*, the FDIC prepares financial statements in accordance with standards promulgated by the Financial Accounting Standards Board (FASB). These statements do not include reporting for assets and liabilities of receivership entities because these entities are legally separate and distinct, and the FRF does not have any ownership interests in them. Periodic and final accountability reports of receivership entities are furnished to courts, supervisory authorities, and others upon request.

USE OF ESTIMATES
Management makes estimates and assumptions that affect the amounts reported in the financial statements and accompanying notes. Actual results could differ from these estimates. Where it is reasonably possible that changes in estimates will cause a material change in the financial statements in the near term, the nature and extent of such changes in estimates have been disclosed. The more significant estimates include the allowance for losses on receivables from thrift resolutions and the estimated losses for litigation.

2

FRF

CASH EQUIVALENTS
Cash equivalents are short term, highly liquid investments consisting primarily of U.S. Treasury Overnight Certificates.

PROVISION FOR LOSSES
The provision for losses represents the change in the estimation of the allowance for losses related to the receivables from thrift resolutions and other assets.

RELATED PARTIES
The nature of related parties and a description of related party transactions are discussed in Note 1 and disclosed throughout the financial statements and footnotes.

DISCLOSURE ABOUT RECENT RELEVANT ACCOUNTING PRONOUNCEMENTS
Recent accounting pronouncements have been deemed to be not applicable or material to the financial statements as presented.

3. Receivables from Thrift Resolutions and Other Assets, Net

RECEIVABLES FROM THRIFT RESOLUTIONS
The receivables from thrift resolutions include payments made by the FRF to cover obligations to insured depositors, advances to receiverships for working capital, and administrative expenses paid on behalf of receiverships. Any related allowance for loss represents the difference between the funds advanced and/or obligations incurred and the expected repayment. Assets held by the FDIC in its receivership capacity for the former RTC are a significant source of repayment of the FRF's receivables from thrift resolutions. As of December 31, 2012, three of the 850 FRF receiverships remain active until their liability related impediments are resolved.

The FRF receiverships held assets with a book value of $13 million and $15 million as of December 31, 2012 and 2011, respectively (which primarily consist of cash held for non FRF, third party creditors).

OTHER ASSETS
Other assets decreased by $59 million to $3 million primarily due to the collection of a receivable for tax benefits sharing of $44 million and the release of the credit enhancement reserves of $13 million (see Note 4, Contingent Liabilities for: Guarantees). The tax benefits sharing collection represented the FRF's share of tax savings by entities that either entered into assistance agreements with the former FSLIC, or have subsequently purchased financial institutions that had prior agreements with the FSLIC.

3

FRF

Receivables from Thrift Resolutions and Other Assets, Net at December 31

DOLLARS IN THOUSANDS

	2012	2011
Receivables from closed thrifts	$ 869,917	$ 1,800,417
Allowance for losses	(867,208)	(1,797,154)
Receivables from Thrift Resolutions, Net	**2,709**	**3,263**
Other assets	2,747	61,900
Total	$ 5,456	$ 65,163

4. Contingent Liabilities for:

GOODWILL LITIGATION

In *United States v. Winstar Corp.*, 518 U.S. 839 (1996), the Supreme Court held that when it became impossible following the enactment of FIRREA in 1989 for the federal government to perform certain agreements to count goodwill toward regulatory capital, the plaintiffs were entitled to recover damages from the United States.

On July 22, 1998, the Department of Justice's (DOJ's) Office of Legal Counsel (OLC) concluded that the FRF is legally available to satisfy all judgments and settlements in the goodwill litigation involving supervisory action or assistance agreements. OLC determined that nonperformance of these agreements was a contingent liability that was transferred to the FRF on August 9, 1989, upon the dissolution of the FSLIC. On July 23, 1998, the U.S. Treasury determined, based on OLC's opinion, that the FRF is the appropriate source of funds for payments of any such judgments and settlements. The FDIC General Counsel concluded that, as liabilities transferred on August 9, 1989, these contingent liabilities for future nonperformance of prior agreements with respect to supervisory goodwill were transferred to the FRF FSLIC, which is that portion of the FRF encompassing the obligations of the former FSLIC. The FRF RTC, which encompasses the obligations of the former RTC and was created upon the termination of the RTC on December 31, 1995, is not available to pay any settlements or judgments arising out of the goodwill litigation.

The FRF can draw from an appropriation provided by Section 110 of the Department of Justice Appropriations Act, 2000 (Public Law 106 113, Appendix A, Title I, 113 Stat. 1501A 3, 1501A 20) such sums as may be necessary for the payment of judgments and compromise settlements in the goodwill litigation. This appropriation is to remain available until expended. Because an appropriation is available to pay such judgments and settlements, any estimated liability for goodwill litigation should have a corresponding receivable from the U.S. Treasury and therefore have no net impact on the financial condition of the FRF.

For the year ended December 31, 2012, the FRF paid $181 million as a result of a settlement in one goodwill case compared to $50 million for one goodwill case in 2011. The FRF received appropriations from the U.S. Treasury to fund these payments.

As of December 31, 2012, two remaining cases are active and pending against the United States based on alleged breaches of the agreements stated above. Of these two remaining cases, a contingent liability and an offsetting receivable of $356 million was recorded for one case as

4

FRF

of December 31, 2012 and 2011. This case is currently before the lower court pending remand following appeal. It is reasonably possible that for this case the FRF could incur additional estimated losses of $63 million, representing additional damages contended by the plaintiff. For the other remaining active case, no awards were given to the plaintiffs by the appellate court. This case is fully adjudicated but the Court of Federal Claims is considering awarding litigation costs to the United States.

At December 31, 2011, there were five active cases. For three of the cases considered active at year end 2011, one was settled and paid during 2012 and two were fully adjudicated with no award; in one of these two cases the Court of Federal Claims awarded litigation costs of $231 thousand to the United States, which was paid in 2012.

In addition, the FRF FSLIC pays the goodwill litigation expenses incurred by the DOJ, the entity that defends these lawsuits against the United States, based on a Memorandum of Understanding (MOU) dated October 2, 1998, between the FDIC and the DOJ. FRF FSLIC pays in advance the estimated goodwill litigation expenses. Any unused funds are carried over and applied toward the next fiscal year (FY) charges. In 2012, FRF FSLIC did not provide any additional funding to the DOJ because the unused funds from prior fiscal years were sufficient to cover estimated FY 2013 expenses.

GUARINI LITIGATION
Paralleling the goodwill cases were similar cases alleging that the government breached agreements regarding tax benefits associated with certain FSLIC assisted acquisitions. These agreements allegedly contained the promise of tax deductions for losses incurred on the sale of certain thrift assets purchased by plaintiffs from the FSLIC, even though the FSLIC provided the plaintiffs with tax exempt reimbursement. A provision in the Omnibus Budget Reconciliation Act of 1993 (popularly referred to as the "Guarini legislation") eliminated the tax deductions for these losses.

All eight of the original Guarini cases have been settled. However, a case settled in 2006 further obligates the FRF FSLIC as a guarantor for all tax liabilities in the event the settlement amount is determined by tax authorities to be taxable. The maximum potential exposure under this guarantee is approximately $81 million. However, the FDIC believes that it is very unlikely the settlement will be subject to taxation. More definitive information may be available during 2013, after the Internal Revenue Service (IRS) completes its Large Case Program audit on the affected entity's 2006 returns; this audit remains ongoing. As of December 31, 2012, no liability has been recorded. The FRF does not expect to fund any payment under this guarantee.

GUARANTEES
On May 21, 2012, the FDIC, in its capacity as manager of the FRF, entered into an agreement with Fannie Mae for the release of $13 million of credit enhancement reserves to the FRF in exchange for indemnifying Fannie Mae for all future losses incurred on 76 multi family mortgage loans. The former RTC supplied Fannie Mae with the credit enhancement reserves in the form of cash collateral to cover future losses on these mortgage loans through 2020. The maximum exposure on this indemnification is the current unpaid principal balance of the remaining 73 multi family loans totaling $10 million. Based on a contingent liability assessment of this portfolio, the average loan to value ratio is 21%, the majority of the loans

5

FRF

are at least 60% amortized, and all are scheduled to mature within three to eight years. Since all of the loans are currently in performing status and no losses have occurred since 2001, future payments on this indemnification are not expected. As a result, the FRF has not recorded a contingent liability for this indemnification as of December 31, 2012.

5. Resolution Equity

As stated in the Overview section of Note 1, the FRF is comprised of two distinct pools: the FRF FSLIC and the FRF RTC. The FRF FSLIC consists of the assets and liabilities of the former FSLIC. The FRF RTC consists of the assets and liabilities of the former RTC. Pursuant to legal restrictions, the two pools are maintained separately and the assets of one pool are not available to satisfy obligations of the other.

The following table shows the contributed capital, accumulated deficit, and resulting resolution equity for each pool.

Resolution Equity at December 31, 2012

DOLLARS IN THOUSANDS

		FRF-FSLIC		FRF-RTC		FRF Consolidated
Contributed capital - beginning	$	46,126,319	$	81,749,337	$	127,875,656
Add: U.S. Treasury payment for goodwill litigation		181,000		0		181,000
Contributed capital - ending		**46,307,319**		**81,749,337**		**128,056,656**
Accumulated deficit		(42,882,341)		(81,577,294)		(124,459,635)
Total	$	**3,424,978**	$	**172,043**	$	**3,597,021**

CONTRIBUTED CAPITAL

The FRF FSLIC and the former RTC received $43.5 billion and $60.1 billion from the U.S. Treasury, respectively, to fund losses from thrift resolutions prior to July 1, 1995. Additionally, the FRF FSLIC issued $670 million in capital certificates to the Financing Corporation (a mixed ownership government corporation established to function solely as a financing vehicle for the FSLIC) and the RTC issued $31.3 billion of these instruments to the REFCORP. FIRREA prohibited the payment of dividends on any of these capital certificates.

FRF FSLIC received $181 million in U.S. Treasury payments for goodwill litigation in 2012. Furthermore, $356 million was accrued for as receivables as of December 31, 2012 and 2011. Through December 31, 2012, the FRF has received or established a receivable for a total of $2.2 billion of goodwill appropriations, the effect of which increases contributed capital.

Through December 31, 2012, the FRF RTC has returned $4.6 billion to the U.S. Treasury and made payments of $5.0 billion to the REFCORP. These actions serve to reduce contributed capital. The most recent payment to the REFCORP was in January of 2008 for $225 million.

ACCUMULATED DEFICIT

The accumulated deficit represents the cumulative excess of expenses and losses over revenue for activity related to the FRF FSLIC and the FRF RTC. Approximately $29.8 billion and

6

FRF

$87.9 billion were brought forward from the former FSLIC and the former RTC on August 9, 1989, and January 1, 1996, respectively. The FRF FSLIC accumulated deficit has increased by $13.1 billion, whereas the FRF RTC accumulated deficit has decreased by $6.3 billion, since their dissolution dates.

6. Disclosures about the Fair Value of Financial Instruments

The following table presents the FRF's financial assets measured at fair value on a recurring basis as of December 31, 2012 and 2011.

Assets Measured at Fair Value at December 31, 2012

DOLLARS IN THOUSANDS

| | Fair Value Measurements Using | | | |
	Quoted Prices in Active Markets for Identical Assets (Level 1)	Significant Other Observable Inputs (Level 2)	Significant Unobservable Inputs (Level 3)	Total Assets at Fair Value
Assets				
Cash equivalents[1]	$ 3,425,097			$ 3,425,097
Total Assets	**$ 3,425,097**	**$ 0**	**$ 0**	**$ 3,425,097**

(1) Cash equivalents are Special U.S. Treasury Certificates with overnight maturities valued at prevailing interest rates established by the U.S. Bureau of Public Debt. Cash equivalents are included in the "Cash and cash equivalents" line item.

Assets Measured at Fair Value at December 31, 2011

DOLLARS IN THOUSANDS

| | Fair Value Measurements Using | | | |
	Quoted Prices in Active Markets for Identical Assets (Level 1)	Significant Other Observable Inputs (Level 2)	Significant Unobservable Inputs (Level 3)	Total Assets at Fair Value
Assets				
Cash equivalents[1]	$ 3,377,203			$ 3,377,203
Credit enhancement reserves[2]		$ 14,431		14,431
Total Assets	**$ 3,377,203**	**$ 14,431**	**$ 0**	**$ 3,391,634**

(1) Cash equivalents are Special U.S. Treasury Certificates with overnight maturities valued at prevailing interest rates established by the U.S. Bureau of Public Debt. Cash equivalents are included in the "Cash and cash equivalents" line item.

(2) Credit enhancement reserves are valued by performing projected cash flow analyses using market-based assumptions.

Some of the FRF's financial assets and liabilities are not recognized at fair value but are recorded at amounts that approximate fair value due to their short maturities and/or comparability with current interest rates. Such items include other short term receivables and accounts payable and other liabilities.

The net receivable from thrift resolutions is influenced by the underlying valuation of receivership assets. This corporate receivable is unique and the estimate presented is not necessarily indicative of the amount that could be realized in a sale to the private sector. Such a sale would require indeterminate, but substantial, discounts for an interested party to profit

7

FRF

from these assets because of credit and other risks. Consequently, it is not practicable to estimate its fair value.

8

Comments from the Federal Deposit Insurance Corporation

Federal Deposit Insurance Corporation
550 17th Street NW, Washington, D.C. 20429-9990   Deputy to the Chairman and CFO

February 14, 2013

Mr. James Dalkin
Director, Financial Management and Assurance
U.S. Government Accountability Office
441 G Street, NW
Washington, DC 20548

Re: FDIC Management Response on the GAO 2012 Financial Statements Audit Report

Dear Mr. Dalkin:

Thank you for the opportunity to review and comment on the U.S. Government Accountability Office's (GAO's) draft report titled, **Financial Audit: Federal Deposit Insurance Corporation Funds' 2012 and 2011 Financial Statements**, GAO-13-291. We are pleased that the Federal Deposit Insurance Corporation (FDIC) has received unmodified (unqualified) opinions for the twenty-first consecutive year on the financial statements of its funds: the Deposit Insurance Fund (DIF) and the FSLIC Resolution Fund (FRF). Also, GAO reported that the FDIC had effective internal control over financial reporting and that there was no reportable noncompliance with provisions of laws and regulations that were tested. Additionally, FDIC is pleased that GAO acknowledged our efforts to resolve the prior year significant control deficiency related to estimating losses to the DIF from shared-loss agreements.

During the audit year, the FDIC management and staff continued to take steps to strengthen and improve the internal control environment and will continue to focus on this area in the coming audit year. FDIC recognizes the important role a strong internal control program plays in an agency achieving its mission. Our dedication to sound financial management has been and will remain a top priority.

In complying with audit standards that require management to provide a written assertion about the effectiveness of its internal control over financial reporting, the FDIC has prepared **Management's Report on Internal Control over Financial Reporting** (see attachment). The report acknowledges management's responsibility for establishing and maintaining internal control over financial reporting and provides the FDIC's conclusion regarding the effectiveness of its internal control.

We want to thank the GAO staff for their professionalism and dedication during the audit and look forward to a productive and successful relationship during the 2013 audit. If you have any questions or concerns, please do not hesitate to contact me.

Sincerely,

Steven O. App

Steven O. App
Deputy to the Chairman
  and Chief Financial Officer

Attachment

Management's Report on Internal Control over Financial Reporting

The Federal Deposit Insurance Corporation's (FDIC's) internal control over financial reporting is a process effected by those charged with governance, management, and other personnel, designed to provide reasonable assurance regarding the preparation of reliable financial statements in accordance with U.S. generally accepted accounting principles (GAAP), and compliance with applicable laws and regulations.

The objective of the FDIC's internal control over financial reporting is to reasonably assure that (1) transactions are properly recorded, processed and summarized to permit the preparation of financial statements in accordance with GAAP, and assets are safeguarded against loss from unauthorized acquisition, use, or disposition; and (2) transactions are executed in accordance with the laws and regulations that could have a direct and material effect on the financial statements.

Management is responsible for establishing and maintaining effective internal control over financial reporting. Management assessed the effectiveness of the FDIC's internal control over financial reporting as of December 31, 2012 through its corporate risk management program that seeks to comply with the spirit of the following standards, among others: Federal Managers' Financial Integrity Act of 1982 (FMFIA); Chief Financial Officers Act (CFO Act); Government Performance and Results Act (GPRA); Federal Information Security Management Act (FISMA); and OMB Circular A-123. In addition, other standards that the FDIC considers are the framework set forth by the Committee of Sponsoring Organizations of the Treadway Commission's *Internal Control - Integrated Framework* and the U.S. Government Accountability Office's (GAO's) *Standards for Internal Control in the Federal Government*.

Based on the above assessment, management concluded that, as of December 31, 2012, FDIC's internal control over financial reporting is effective based upon the criteria established in FMFIA.

Federal Deposit Insurance Corporation
February 14, 2013